ANSWERS

to the questions
on the back cover

A: The 12:50, because it's 10 to 1 if you catch it.

B: Because each player raises a racket.

C: A penny.

D: Simply spellbound.

E: Get water from the bed springs and dates from the calendar.

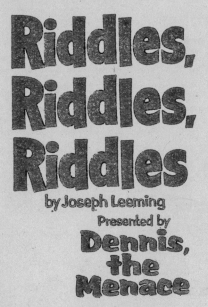

Riddles, Riddles, Riddles

by Joseph Leeming

Presented by

Dennis, the Menace

Drawings by Hank Ketcham

FAWCETT GOLD MEDAL • NEW YORK

RIDDLES, RIDDLES, RIDDLES

**THIS BOOK CONTAINS THE COMPLETE TEXT OF THE
ORIGINAL HARDCOVER EDITION.**

A Fawcett Gold Medal Book reprinted by arrangement with
Franklin Watts, Inc., and Hank Ketcham

Copyright © 1955 by Post-Hall Syndicate, Inc.
Copyright 1954 by Post-Hall Syndicate and Henry Ketcham
Copyright © 1955, 1957, 1958, 1959, 1961, 1962, 1963 by
The Hall Syndicate, Inc.
Copyright © 1961, 1960, 1959, 1954 by Hank Ketcham
Copyright 1953 by Franklin Watts, Inc.

© 1967 CBS Publications, The Consumer Publishing
Division of CBS, Inc. All Rights Reserved.

Cover drawing Copyright © 1967 by Hank Ketcham

ISBN: 0-449-14014-8

Printed in the United States of America

26 25 24 23 22 21 20 19 18 17

FOREWORD

Everyone loves riddles. They are often the quickest and funniest jokes in the world. In a split second a clever riddle will jolt even a deadpan into uncontrollable laughter.

After a good deal of serious study, I have come to the conclusion that the main trouble with riddles is that no one knows enough of them! This was proved when I was collecting riddles for this book. Whenever I could, I tried out riddles to see if they were as funny as I thought they were. Over and over again, my unsuspecting victims looked blank for a second or two, then burst into guffaws of laughter. To my great delight, most of these poor guinea pigs had never before heard the riddles I sprang on them. I hope that you, dear reader, will find them just as fresh.

Oddly enough, hardly anyone seems to know the difference between a riddle and a conundrum. A riddle is a question to which the answer, while unexpected, is pretty straightforward. For example: "What can be heard and caught but never seen?" The answer is: "A remark."

Conundrums, on the other hand, are based on double meanings or plays on words. Hundreds of these puns are so outrageous that they would make the shaggiest of shaggy dogs howl, tear up the ground with his paws, and run away and hide for shame. An example of a not-too-shaggy kind would be: "What is the difference between a mouse and a pretty girl?" The answer: "One harms the cheese, the other charms the he's."

Independent research, however, has shown that really shaggy conundrums split more sides than do cautious ones!

Riddles and conundrums are a kind of puzzle, and the answers to many of them can be figured out—after a while. In this book they are told mostly just for fun, and for this reason, the answers are printed right beneath the riddles. It is easier for the reader than looking for the answers in a separate section in the back of the book, and it is done because most people would rather laugh at the answers right away than try to puzzle them out.

JOSEPH LEEMING

1   What kind of shoes are made out of banana skins?
    Slippers.

2   What makes the Tower of Pisa lean?
    It never eats.

3   What colors would you paint the sun and the wind?
    The sun rose and the wind blue.

4   What would happen if a girl should swallow her teaspoon?
    She wouldn't be able to stir.

5   What is the easiest thing for a stingy man to part with?
    A comb.

6   What is the most difficult train to catch?
    The 12:50, because it's 10 to 1 if you catch it.

7   What most resembles half a cheese?
    The other half.

8   What is never of any use unless it is in a tight place?
    A cork.

9   What, besides a good rule, works both ways?
    A ferry boat.

0 What ship has two mates but no captain?
Courtship.

11 What do all ships weigh, regardless of their size?
Their anchors.

12 What man's business is best when things are dullest?
A knife-sharpener.

13 What is always filled when it is used and empty when at rest?
A shoe.

14 What becomes higher when the head is off?
A pillow.

15 What is sure to go out the tighter it is locked in?
A fire.

16 What coat is put on only when it is wet?
A coat of paint.

17 What can be a speaking likeness and yet is dumb?
A photograph.

18 What man can raise things without lifting them?
A farmer.

19 To what man does everyone always take off his hat?
The barber.

20 What tongue can wag and yet never utter a word?
The tongue of your shoe.

21 What does everyone take off last when going to bed?
His feet from the floor.

22 What may have wings, yet not fly?
A house.

23 What kind of boat is like a knife?
A cutter.

24 What musical instrument has the best character?
A piano, because it may be grand, upright or square.

25 What keeps the moon in place?
Its beams.

26 What liquid is like the load a freight ship carries?
Gasoline, because it makes the car go.

27 Why is the Senate like a book?
Because it has so many pages.

28 What time is it when a pie is divided among four hungry boys?
A quarter to one.

29 What cord is always full of knots, not one of which can be untied?
A cord of wood.

30 What kind of clothing lasts the longest?
Underwear, because it is never worn out.

31 What is the keynote of good manners?
B natural.

32 What kind of noise annoys an oyster?
A noisy noise annoys an oyster.

33 What is the right kind of lumber for castles in the air?
Sunbeams.

34 What is the highest pleasure you can think of?
Riding an airplane.

35 What is smaller than an ant's mouth?
What the ant eats.

36 What American has had the largest family?
George Washington, who was the "father of his country."

37   What insect does a blacksmith manufacture?
     He makes the fire-fly.

38   What did the blind man say to the policeman when
     the policeman said he would arrest him if he didn't
     move on?
     I'd just like to see you do it.

39   What do you call a boy who eats all the apples he
     can get, whether they are green or old?
     He is what we might call a pains-taking youngster.

40   What is the smallest bridge in the world?
     The bridge of a nose.

41   What is the highest building in New York?
     The Public Library has the most stories.

42   What does a hen do when it stands on one leg?
     Lifts up the other leg.

43   What is the most indigestible meal you can eat?
     Bolt the door and tuck in the sheets.

44   What part of a fish weighs the most?
     The scales.

45   What is the best way to keep goats from smelling?
     Cut off their noses.

46   What man has eyes in the back of his head?
     The man whose hindsight is better than his fore-
     sight.

47   What do you think is the greatest feat of eating
     ever known?
     The one in which the man began by bolting a
     door, threw up a window, and then sat down and
     swallowed a story whole.

48   **What game do the waves like to play?**
Pitch and toss.

49   **What geometrical figure represents a lost parrot?**
Polygon (polly gone).

50   **What is the best thing to make in a hurry?**
Haste.

51   **What should you do if you split your sides laughing?**
Run fast until you get a stitch in them.

52   **What kind of money do girls like the most?**
Matrimony.

53   **What is the most difficult key to turn?**
A donkey.

54   **What is there about a yardstick that is very remarkable?**
Though it has no head nor tail, it has a foot at each end and another foot in the middle.

55   **What good quality does the North Pole remind you of?**
Justice (Just ice).

56   **What makes the ocean angry?**
It has been crossed so many times.

57   **What is the best thing to put into pies?**
Your teeth.

58   **What makes more noise than a pig caught under a fence?**
Two pigs.

59   **What is worse than finding a worm in an apple?**
Finding half a worm.

60   What great benefit is there in a paper of pins?
It has a lot of good points.

61   What word is usually pronounced wrong, even by the best of scholars?
Wrong, of course.

62   What question is it to which you positively must answer yes?
What does Y-E-S spell?

63   What roof never keeps out the wet?
The roof of your mouth.

64   What wind does a hungry sailor like the most?
A wind that blows foul (fowl) and chops about.

65   What is the most contradictory sign seen in a library?
To speak aloud is not allowed (aloud).

66   What is the most disagreeable month for soldiers?
A long March.

67   What is a sure sign of an early spring?
A cat with her back up, watching a hole in the wall.

68   What is the best way to make time go fast?
Use the spur of the moment.

69   What is a well-known put-up job?
The paper on the wall.

70   What is the only thing you can break when you say its name?
Silence.

71   What question can never be answered by "Yes"?
Are you asleep?

72   What relation is the doorstep to the doormat?
A step-father (farther).

73   **What is most like a hen stealin'?**
A cock robin.

74   **What salad is best for newlyweds?**
Lettuce alone.

75   **What is the largest room in the world?**
Room for improvement.

76   **What is the oldest piece of furniture in the world?**
The multiplication table.

77   **What walks over the water and under the water, yet does not touch the water?**
A woman crossing a bridge over a river with a pail of water on her head.

78   **What does a calf become after it is one year old?**
Two years old.

79   **What is the best thing to take when you are run down?**
The number of the car that hit you.

80   **What pets make stirring music?**
Trumpets.

81   **What is the coldest place in a theater?**
Z row (zero).

82   **What fishes have eyes nearest together?**
The smallest fishes.

83   **What does a person usually grow in a garden if he works hard?**
Tired.

84   **What happens to a cat when it crosses a desert on Christmas Day?**
It gets sandy claws (Santa Claus).

85 **What did the big firecracker say to the little firecracker?**
"My pop's bigger than your pop."

86 **What is the hardest thing about learning to ride a bicycle?**
The pavement.

87 **What is the end of everything?**
The letter G.

88 **What room can no one enter?**
A mushroom.

89 **What driver never gets arrested?**
A screwdriver.

90 **What is there in your house that ought to be looked into?**
A mirror.

91 **What coin is double its value when half is deducted?**
Half a dollar.

92 **What is the surest way to double your money?**
Fold it.

93 **What is the best and cheapest light?**
Daylight.

94 **What goes through a door, but never goes in or comes out?**
A keyhole.

95 **What did Paul Revere say when he finished his famous ride?**
"Whoa."

96 **What fish may be said to be out of place?**
A perch in a bird cage.

97   **What has a hand but can't scratch itself?**
A clock.

98   **What sort of necktie would a smart pig choose?**
A pig's tie (pigsty).

99   **What intelligent insect do you find in schoolrooms?**
Spelling bees.

100   **What flies up but still is down?**
A feather.

101   **What is the richest country in the world?**
Ireland, because its capital is always Dublin.

102   **What does the garden say when it laughs?**
"Hoe, hoe, hoe!"

103   **What would you call a man who is always wiring for money?**
An electrician.

104   **What letter in the Dutch alphabet will name a titled lady?**
A Dutch-ess.

105   **What musical instrument should we never believe?**
A lyre.

106   **What soap is the hardest?**
Castile (cast steel).

107   **What are the most difficult ships to conquer?**
Hardships.

108   **What is a hot time?**
A clock in an oven.

109   **What is the worst weather for rats and mice?**
When it rains cats and dogs.

HOW MANY FISH CAN YOU CATCH?

Here are thirty well-known fish, with a good clue given for each one. How many of them can you catch?

1   What is a struggling fish?
2   What is a cheating fish given to sharp practices?
3   What is a fish of precious metal?
4   What fish is man's best friend?
5   What fish is a royal fish?
6   What fish is a heavenly fish?
7   What fish is in the band?
8   What fish is an animal that is almost extinct?
9   What fish is an ugly old witch?
10   What fish is a household pet?
11   What fish do you find in a bird cage?
12   What fish is good with hot biscuits?
13   What fish is a sharp-pointed weapon that soldiers used in Robin Hood's time?
14   What fish is a member of a barber shop quartet?
15   What fish is a deep guttural sound?
16   What fish is used on certain boats?
17   What fish is very useful in hot weather?
18   What fish is used by a fencer?
19   What fish is seen at night?
20   What poor fish is always ailing?
21   What fish makes a good sandwich?
22   What fish is a very evil fish?
23   What fish is a very dark color?

24 What fish floats through the air?
25 What fish is a favorite with dairy farmers?
26 What fish is a rosy biter?
27 What fish represents three letters used by stores delivering goods you buy?
28 What fish represents a process used in refining metals?
29 What is a gloomy, down-in-the-mouth fish?
30 What fish warms the earth?

1 Flounder   2 Shark   3 Goldfish   4 Dogfish
5 Kingfish 6 Angelfish 7 Drumfish 8 Buffalo fish
9 Hagfish 10 Catfish 11 Perch 12 Butterfish
13 Pike   14 Bass   15 Grunt   20 Sailfish
17 Fantail 18 Swordfish 19 Starfish 20 Weakfish
21 Jellyfish   22 Devilfish   23 Blackfish
24 Balloon fish   25 Cowfish   26 Red snapper
27 Cod (C.O.D.) 28 Smelt 29 Bluefish 30 Sunfish

PLEASE TELL ME WHY?

1 **Why should you never tell secrets in a cornfield?**
Because corn has ears and is bound to be shocked.

2 **Why do you always make a mistake when you put on a shoe?**
Because you put your foot in it.

3 **Why does Santa Claus like to go down the chimney?**
Because it suits (soots) him.

4 **Why do white sheep eat more than black ones?**
Because there are more of them in the world.

5 **Why is a ship one of the most polite things on earth?**
Because it always advances with a bow.

6 **Why is the snow different from Sunday?**
Because it can fall on any day of the week.

7 **Why is a good student always on the run?**
Because he is always pursuing his studies.

8 **Why does a man who has just shaved look like a wild animal?**
Because he has a bear face.

9 Why should watermelon be a good name for a newspaper?
   Because we're sure it is red on the inside.

10 Why is it vulgar to sing and play by yourself?
   Because such a performance is so low (solo).

11 Why can't it rain for two days continually?
   Because there is always a night in between.

12 Why does an Indian wear feathers in his hair?
   To keep his wigwam.

13 Why is your nose in the middle of your face?
   Because it is a scenter (center).

14 Why should fish be well educated?
   Because they are so often found in schools.

15 Why should you expect a fisherman to be more honest than a shepherd?
   Because a fisherman lives by hook and a shepherd lives by crook.

16 Why is your sense of touch impaired when you are ill?
   Because you don't feel well.

17 Why do carpenters believe there is no such thing as glass?
   Because they never saw it.

18 Why should a lost traveler never starve in the middle of a desert?
   Because of the sand which is (sandwiches) there.

19 Why are photographers the most progressive of men?
   Because they are always developing.

20 Why is coffee like a dull knife?
   Because it has to be ground before it can be used.

21 Why is tennis such a noisy game?
Because each player raises a racket.

22 Why should everyone go to sleep immediately after drinking a cup of tea?
Because when the T is gone, night is nigh.

23 Why is an orange like a church belfry?
Because we get a peel (peal) from it.

24 Why are weary people like automobile wheels?
Because they are tired.

25 Why is a river rich?
Because it always has two banks.

26 Why does the tightrope dancer always have to repeat his performance?
Because he is always on cord (encored).

27 Why do we all go to bed?
Because the bed won't come to us.

28 Why can't a tugboat in New York Harbor go in a straight line?
Because some tow (toe) in, and others tow out.

29 Why should taxicab drivers be brave men?
Because "none but the brave deserve the fair (fare)."

30 Why does a chicken cross the road?
To get to the other side.

31 Why does a coat get bigger when you take it out of a suitcase?
Because you will find it increases (in creases).

32 Why do we buy clothes?
Because we can't get them for nothing.

33   **Why is coal the most contradictory thing that is bought and sold?**
Because when it is bought, instead of going to the buyer, it goes to the cellar.

34   **Why is it that every man's trousers are too short?**
Because his legs always stick out two feet.

35   **Why should a doctor never be seasick?**
Because he is so accustomed to sea (see) sickness.

36   **Why does a tall man eat less than a short man?**
Because he makes a little go a long way.

37   **Why is a doctor the meanest man on earth?**
Because he treats you and then makes you pay for it.

38   **Why doesn't a steam locomotive like to sit down?**
Because it has a tender behind.

39   **Why are fat men sad?**
Because they are men of sighs (size).

40   **Why are fishermen such wonderful correspondents?**
Because they always like to drop a line.

41   **Why is a fly one of the grocer's best customers?**
Because when he comes for sugar, he settles on the spot.

42   **Why is a gardener the most extraordinary man in the world?**
Because he has more business on earth than any other man; he has good grounds for what he does; he is master of the mint; he sets his own time (thyme); he has more bows (boughs) than the President of the United States; and better still, he can raise his own salary (celery) every year.

43   **Why are tall people always the laziest?**
Because they are longer in bed than short people.

44 **Why does lightning shock people?**
Because it doesn't know how to conduct itself.

45 **Why is it impossible for a person who lisps to believe in the existence of young ladies?**
Because with him every miss is a myth.

46 **Why is it that when you are looking for something you always find it in the last place you look?**
Because you always stop looking when you find it.

47 **Why don't women become bald as soon as men?**
Because they wear their hair longer.

48 **Why is paper money more valuable than coins?**
When you put it in your pocket you double it, and when you take it out you find it still in creases.

49 **Why can a bride hide nothing?**
Because somebody always gives her away.

50 **Why is it useless to send a telegram to Washington today?**
Because he is dead.

51 **Why should a fisherman always be wealthy?**
Because all his business is net profit.

52 **Why is life the hardest riddle?**
Because everybody has to give it up.

53 **Why is a heavy fall of snow easy to understand?**
Because you can always see the drift of it.

54 **Why does a bald-headed man have no use for keys?**
Because he has lost his locks.

55 **Why should you never swim in the River Seine, at Paris?**
Because, if you did, you would be insane (in Seine).

56 Why should you expect a fire in a circus to be very destructive?
Because it is intense (in tents).

57 Why should a dishonest man always stay indoors?
So no one will ever find him out.

53 Why should a spider make a good outfielder?
Because it is always catching flies.

59 Why can hens lay eggs only during the day?
Because at night they become roosters.

60 Why should you be careful about telling secrets in the country?
Because the corn has ears, the potatoes have eyes, and the beans talk (beanstalk).

61 Why is handwriting in ink like a dead pig?
Because it is done with a pen.

62 Why does a Model-T Ford remind you of a schoolroom?
Because it has a lot of little nuts, with a crank up front.

63 Why does time fly?
Because so many people are trying to kill it.

64 Why is a hungry man willing to be a martyr?
Because he is more than ready to go to the stake (steak).

65 Why did Babe Ruth make so much money?
Because a good batter always makes good dough.

66 Why is a pig the most unusual animal in the world?
Because he is killed before he is cured.

67 Why did Bill's mother knit him three stockings when he was in the army?
Because Bill wrote her he had gotten so tall he had grown another foot.

68 Why is the inside of everything so mysterious?
Because we can't make it out.

69 Why should ladies who wish to remain slender avoid the letter C?
Because it makes fat a fact.

70 Why do children object to the absence of Santa Claus?
Because they prefer his presence (presents).

71 Why does a warm day give an icicle a bad reputation?
Because it turns it into an eavesdropper.

72 Why does the Statue of Liberty stand in New York Harbor?
Because it can't sit down.

73 Why is autumn the best time for a lazy person to read a book?
Because autumn turns the leaves for him.

74 Why is a policeman the strongest man in the world?
Because he can hold up automobiles with one hand.

75 Why did John tiptoe past the medicine chest?
Because he was afraid he'd awaken the sleeping pills.

76 Why is a tailor a very fine lover?
Because he is an expert at pressing a suit.

77 Why did the jelly roll?
It saw the apple turnover.

78 Why is your nose not twelve inches long?
Because then it would be a foot.

79 Why is the position of President of the United States like a back tooth?
Because it is hard to fill.

80 **Why is an empty purse always the same?**
Because there is never any change in it.

81 **Why are passengers in airplanes so polite to each other?**
For fear of falling out.

82 **Why is a crown prince like a cloudy day?**
Because he is likely to reign.

83 **Why would a barber rather shave six men from New York than one from Kokomo?**
Because he would get six <u>times</u> as much money.

84 **Why does a cook wear a high white hat?**
To cover his head.

85 **Why is an empty matchbox superior to all others?**
Because it is matchless.

86 **Why is a coward like a leaky faucet?**
Because they both run.

87 **Why can you call a horse the most negative of all the animals?**
Because he always neighs (nays).

88 **Why does a cat look first to one side and then to the other when it enters a room?**
Because it can't see both sides at once.

89 **Why is the tongue like an unhappy girl?**
Because they are both down in the mouth.

WHAT AM I?

1. I am something that never asks any questions, but I demand a great many answers. What am I?
A doorbell.

2 I am something that can run and whistle, but can neither walk nor talk. What am I?
A railroad engine.

3 I am something that can be heard and caught, but never seen. What am I?
A remark.

4 I am something everyone tends to overlook no matter how careful he is. What am I?
Your nose.

5 I am something that is lighter than a feather, and yet harder to hold. What am I?
Your breath.

6 I am something that is often found where I don't exist. What am I?
Fault.

7 I am something that always increases the more I am shared with others. What am I?
Happiness.

8   I am something that is too much for one, enough for two, but nothing at all for three. What am I?
     A secret.

9   Use me well, I'm everybody; scratch my back, and I'm nobody. What am I?
     A mirror.

10   I am taken from a mine and shut up in a wooden case from which I am never released, and yet I am used by nearly everybody. What am I?
     The lead in a pencil.

11   Take away my first letter; take away my second letter; take away all my letters, and I remain the same. What am I?
     The postman.

12   Those who have me not, do not wish for me. Those who have me do not wish to lose me. Those who win me have me no longer. What am I?
     A lawsuit.

13   I am forever, and yet was never. What am I?
     Eternity.

14   I'm a part of a chain. Change my first letter and I become a color. Change my first letter again and I am a place where people go to skate. Change my first letter again and I am an entanglement. Change it again and I become a fur-bearing animal. Give me a different first letter and I am found in the kitchen. Change my first letter again and I am a motion of the eye. What am I?
     Link, pink, rink, kink, mink, sink, wink.

15   I occur once in every minute, twice in every moment, and yet not once in a hundred thousand years. What am I?
     The letter M.

16   You can hang me on the wall, but if you take me down, you can't hang me up again. What am I?
Wallpaper.

17   I am something that everyone holds once in a while, but hardly anyone touches me. What am I?
The tongue.

18   I am something that always weighs the same, whether I am larger or smaller. What am I?
A hole.

19   I am something that makes everything visible, but am myself unseen. What am I?
Light.

20   I am something that always goes around a button. What am I?
A goat. A goat always goes around a-buttin'.

21   I am something that is known all over the world, and I have a name of three letters. Strangely enough, when two of my letters are taken away, I still have the same name. What am I?
Tea.

22   I am something that comes with a train, goes with a train, is of no use to the train, and yet the train can't go without me. What am I?
Noise.

23   I am something that has never been felt, seen, nor heard; never existed; and yet I have a name. What am I?
Nothing.

24   I am something that has four legs and only one foot. What am I?
A bed.

25 I am something that one man can carry, but a hundred men can't stand on end. What am I?
A rope.

26 I am something that can run but can't walk. What am I?
Water.

27 I am something that has form and size and can be seen, yet I cannot be felt, and I have neither substance nor weight. What am I?
A shadow.

28 I am something that every living person has seen, but no one will ever see me again. What am I?
Yesterday.

29 I am something that a girl often looks for, but always hopes she won't find. What am I?
A run in her stocking.

30 I am something that is full of holes and yet can hold water. What am I?
A sponge.

31 I am something that is filled every morning and emptied every night, except once a year when I am filled at night and emptied in the morning. What am I?
A stocking.

32 I am something that no man wants, yet no man wants to lose. What am I?
A bald head.

33 I am something that has teeth, but can't eat. What am I?
A comb.

34 I am something that no one has ever seen, but many have heard me, and I won't speak unless I'm spoken to. What am I?
An echo.

35   I am something that grows stronger, instead of weaker, the older I get. What am I?
    Butter.

36   I am something that has three feet and yet I am unable to walk. What am I?
    A yardstick.

37   I am something that has a head and a tail, but no body. What am I?
    A penny.

THE
RIDDLE
OF THE
SPHINX

The Riddle of the Sphinx is probably the oldest of all riddles. It appears in ancient Greek mythology.

The Sphinx, a monster with a human head and the body of a beast, sat on a high rock by the roadside near the city of Thebes, in Egypt. To everyone who passed by she asked the following riddle:

"What is it that has but one voice, and goes first on four feet, then on two, and lastly on three?"

All who could not solve the riddle were strangled by the Sphinx and then thrown down from the high rock. For a long time nobody could guess the answer, and a great many people were killed.

Finally, Oedipus, the son of the king of Thebes, came along the road and was stopped by the Sphinx. The Sphinx asked him the famous riddle.

Said Oedipus, "The answer to your riddle is 'a man.'"

"What makes you think that?" demanded the Sphinx.

"Because a man crawls on all fours as an infant, then walks erect on two feet, and in his old age uses a staff or a cane," Oedipus replied.

This was indeed the right answer. The Sphinx was so furious when her riddle was solved that she threw herself down from the high rock and perished. But her riddle has lasted throughout the centuries, and still puzzles a lot of people, even today.

SOME (SHAGGY) DOG RIDDLES

1   Why does a dog turn around three times before lying down?
    Because one good turn deserves another.

2   Plant a puppy and what would come up?
    Why, dogwood (dog would), doggone it.

3   What is the difference between a dog's tail and a rich man?
    One keeps a waggin' (wagon), and the other keeps two or three big automobiles.

4   Why is a dog's tail like the heart of a tree?
    Because it's farthest from the bark.

5   Why is a hill like a lazy dog?
    Because a hill is an inclined plane; an inclined plane is a slope up (slow pup); and a slow pup is a lazy dog.

6   Why is a dog longer in the morning than in the evening?
    Because he is let out in the morning and taken in in the evening.

7   A mother asked her daughter one day, "Susie, why is Rover like a religious creed?"
    Susie was no dope. She was a pretty smart kid and

answered right back, "Because he's a dog, Ma (dogma)."

8   **When the doctor looks at a dog's lungs with an X-ray, what do you think he finds?**
    The seat of his pants.

9   **When you look into a dog's mouth, what do you sometimes find?**
    The seat of someone else's pants.

10 **Why does a dog wear more clothes in summer than in winter?**
    Because in winter he wears a coat, but in summer he wears a coat, and pants too.

11 **When is a dog's tail not a dog's tail?**
    When it's a wagon (waggin').

12 **Why is a dog biting his own tail like a good manager?**
    Because he makes both ends meet.

13 **When is a dog most like a human being?**
    When he's between a man and a boy.

14 **Why is a dog with a lame leg like a schoolboy adding six and seven?**
    Because he puts down three and carries one.

15 **What does a dog have that nothing else has?**
    Puppies.

16 **Why is a dainty little lapdog like a galloping hyena?**
    Because a hyena is a fast, hideous (fastidious) beast.

17 **What makes a pet dog wag his tail when he sees his master?**
    Because he's got one to wag.

18　**What makes a coach dog spotted?**
His spots.

19　**When is a black dog not a black dog?**
When he is a greyhound (some greyhounds are black).

20　**Why is a dog like a tree?**
Because they both produce a bark.

21　**When does a black-and-tan dog change his color?**
When he turns to bay.

22　**What is the difference between a dog losing his hair and a man painting a small building?**
One is shedding his coat, and the other coating his shed.

23　**What garment does a dog put on for fast trips?**
Pants.

24　**What dog keeps the best time?**
A watch dog.

25　**What is more wonderful than a dog that can count?**
A spelling bee.

26　**Why are a shaggy dog and a tree alike?**
Because they both lose their bark when they die.

27　**When is a shaggy dog most likely to enter a house?**
When the door is open.

HOW'S YOUR GEOGRAPHY?

1   What would you do if you found Chicago Ill?
Get a Baltimore MD.

2   When do you get like a well-known South American country?
When you are Chile.

3   Why is Massachusetts like an egg?
Because it has a Hol-yoke.

4   What New York river asks a question, and what Vermont river answers it?
Hoo-sick? Pa-sum-sick.

5   Why is a barefoot boy like an Alaskan Eskimo?
Because he wears no shoes (wears snow shoes).

6   Why doesn't Sweden have to send abroad for cattle?
Because she keeps a good Stockholm (stock home).

7   If Mississ Ippi should lend Miss Ouri her New Jersey, what would Dela Ware?
Al-ask-a (I'll ask her).

8   What was the greatest feat of strength ever performed in the United States?
Wheeling West Virginia.

9   **What state is round at both ends and high in the middle?**
Ohio.

10   **What is the happiest state?**
Merryland (Maryland).

11   **Why is the Isthmus of Suez like the first U in cucumber?**
Because it's between two seas (C's).

12   **What did Tennessee?**
The same thing that Arkansas.

13   **What did Tennessee the next time it looked?**
It saw Ida hoe (Idaho).

14   **If Iowa month's rent, what does Ohio?**
Money for taxes (Texas).

15   **Which was the largest island before Australia was discovered?**
It was Australia, just the same.

16   **What sea would you like to be in on a wet, rainy day?**
Adriatic (a dry attic).

17   **Why do some people think that Noah was born in New Jersey?**
Because he was a New-ark man.

18   **Why is the Mississippi the most talkative of rivers?**
Because it has a dozen mouths.

19   **Why do so many of the Chinese travel on foot?**
Because there is only one Cochin-China (coach in China).

20   **Which of the West Indian islands does a maker of preserved fruits resemble?**
Jamaica (jam-maker).

21   What is it that is found in the very center of America and Australia?
The letter R.

22   Why is the Leaning Tower of Pisa like Greenland?
Because it is oblique (so bleak).

23   Why is a trip to Egypt fit only for very old gentlemen?
Because it's a see-Nile (senile) thing to do.

24   Why is a man hurrying to rescue Hannah from drowning like a man journeying to a well-known southern city?
Because he is going to save Hannah (Savannah).

25   If Ireland should sink, what would float?
Cork.

26   What part of London is in France?
The letter N.

27   What continent do you see when you look in the mirror in the morning?
You see Europe (you're up).

SOME DIFFICULT FEATS (FEETS)

1   What is a foot to get for a barefoot boy?
2   What foot tells you that someone is right behind you?
3   What foot do you find on a page?
4   What foot do you find on a stage?
5   What is a foot that steals things?
6   What foot do you feel after a long walk?
7   What foot is a servant in a castle?
8   What foot does grandma like to have in the living room?
9   What foot is free and a roamer?
10   What foot is an exciting outdoor game?

1 Footwear   2 Footfall   3 Footnote   4 Footlight
5 Footpad   6 Footsore   7 Footman   8 Footstool
9 Footloose   10 Football

WHICH IS WHICH?

1   **Which is the strongest day of the week?**
Sunday, because all the rest are weak days.

2   **Which can move faster, heat or cold?**
Heat, because you can catch cold.

3   **Which is correct: The white of the eggs _is_ yellow, or the white of the eggs _are_ yellow?**
Neither. The whites are never yellow.

4   **Which takes less time to get ready for a trip—an elephant or a rooster?**
The rooster. He takes only his comb, while the elephant has to take a whole trunk.

5   **Which is better—complete happiness or a bread-and-butter sandwich?**
A bread-and-butter sandwich. Nothing is better than complete happiness, and a bread-and-butter sandwich is much better than nothing.

6   **Which has more legs—a horse or no horse?**
No horse. No horse has five or more legs. A horse has just four legs.

7   **Which candles burn longer—wax candles or tallow candles?**
Neither. They both burn shorter.

8   **Which is heavier, milk or cream?**
Milk is, because cream rises to the surface.

9   **Which would you rather have—a lion eat you or a tiger?**
Thanks, I'd rather have the lion eat the tiger.

10   **Which is the most dangerous bat that flies in the air?**
A brickbat.

11   **Which has more legs, a cow or no cow?**
Well, no cow has eight legs, and that is more than most cows have.

12   **Which member of Congress wears the largest hat?**
The one with the largest head.

13   **Which is the left side of a round plum pudding?**
The part that isn't eaten.

14   **Which tree is the most suggestive of romance?**
Yew, dear.

15   **Which is heavier, a half or a full moon?**
The half, because the full moon is as light again as the half moon.

16   **Which of the heavenly bodies has the most small change in its pockets?**
The moon, because it is always changing quarters.

17   **Which is the laziest plant, and which the most active?**
The creeper and the running vine.

18   **Which of your parents is your nearest relative?**
Your mother, because your other parent is always father (farther).

A KENNEL

FULL

OF CURS

1   What cur do you find at the edge of a street?
2   What cur tolls at nighttime?
3   What cur is a religious one?
4   What cur is a healer?
5   What cur is a person in charge of a museum?
6   What cur is full of electricity?
7   What cur is good for making jelly?
8   What cur is the most inquisitive one?
9   What cur hangs at the window?
10 What cur can you spend?
11 What cur is a bird?
12 What cur belongs to a baseball pitcher?

1 Curb   2 Curfew   3 Curate   4 Cure   5 Curator
6 Current 7 Currant 8 Curiosity 9 Curtain 10 Currency 11 Curlew 12 Curve

LOTS
OF
LETTUCE
(LETTERS)

1   **Why is the letter E always discontented?**
Because, while it is never out of health or pocket, it never appears in good spirits.

2   **Why is the letter A like honeysuckle?**
Because a B (bee) is always after it.

3   **Why is the letter D like a bad boy?**
Because it makes ma mad.

4   **Why is O the noisiest of the vowels?**
Because all the other vowels (A, E, I, U) are inaudible (in "audible").

5   **Why do you think B comes before C?**
Because we must be (B) before we can see (C).

6   **What starts with a T, ends with a T, and is full of T?**
A teapot.

7   **What helpful thing does the letter A do for a deaf woman?**
It makes her hear.

8   **What is always invisible yet never out of sight?**
The letters I and S.

9   **Why is the letter F like death?**
Because it makes all fall.

10   **Why is a false friend like the letter P?**
Because he is the first in pity, but the last in help.

11   **Tommy Tucker took two strings and tied two turtles to two tall trees. How many T's are there in that?**
To be perfectly frank, there are only two T's in "that."

12   **What word of only three syllables contains twenty-six letters?**
Alphabet.

13   **Why is a sewing machine like the letter S?**
Because it makes needles needless.

14   **Why is the letter E so unfortunate?**
Because it is always out of cash and always in debt and great danger.

15   **Which two letters of the alphabet have nothing between them?**
N and P have O (nothing) between them.

16   **What letter of the alphabet separates Europe from Africa?**
C (sea).

17   **What four letters of the alphabet would scare off a burglar?**
O, I C U (Oh, I see you).

18   **What is it that every pauper possesses that others have not?**
The letter P.

19   **What is the most important thing in the world?**
The letter E, because it is first in everybody and everything.

20   What letter is always nine inches long?
The letter Y, which is always one-fourth of a yard.

21   What letter is never found in the alphabet?
The one you mail.

22   What letter in the alphabet can travel the greatest distance?
The letter D, because it goes to the end of the world.

23   If all the letters of the alphabet were invited to a luncheon party, what six letters would fail to arrive on time?
The letters U, V, W, X, Y and Z, because they come only after T (tea).

24   What always has at least ten letters in it and may have tens of thousands of letters?
A post office.

25   In what way are the letter O and a neatly kept house alike?
Both are always in order.

26   In what way are the letter A and high noon alike?
Both are in the middle of day.

27   What letter is a drink?
T.

28   What letter is a vegetable?
P.

29   What letter is an insect?
B.

30   What letter is a part of the head?
I.

31   Why is U the jolliest letter?
Because it is always in the midst of fun.

GIRLS
ARE
ALWAYS
RIDDLES

1   **When is a pretty girl like a ship?**
When she's attached to a boy (buoy).

2   **How can a girl best keep a boy's affection?**
By not returning it.

3   **How would it work if all the post offices were in the charge of pretty girls?**
It would work so well that the mails (males) would arrive and depart every hour of the day.

4   **If a pretty girl fell into a well, why couldn't her brother help her out?**
How could he be a brother and assist her (a sister) too?

5   **In what month do girls talk the least?**
In February, because it is the shortest month.

6   **How can you tell a girl named Ellen that she is delightful, in eight letters?**
U-R-A-B-U-T-L-N (You are a beauty, Ellen).

7   **What is the difference between a soldier and a pretty girl?**
One faces the powder, and the other powders the face.

8   Why is a nice but inelegant girl like brown sugar?
    Because she's sweet but unrefined.

9   Why do girls like to look at the moon?
    Because there's a man in it.

10 Why is a proud girl like a music book?
    Because she is full of airs.

11 One boy calls his girl-friend "Postscript." What do
    you think her real name is?
    Adeline Moore (Add a line more).

12 What two beaus can every girl always have near at
    hand?
    Elbows.

13 Why are girls like hinges?
    Because they are things to a door (adore).

14 Why are girls like their own watches?
    Because they are pretty to look at, have delicate
    faces and hands, but are sometimes difficult to regu-
    late when once they get going.

15 What girl is always making blunders?
    Miss Take (mistake).

16 What girls are they whose days are always unlucky?
    Miss Chance, Miss Fortune and Miss Hap.

17 What girls have especially jealous tempers?
    Miss Give and Miss Trust.

18 What are the three quickest ways of spreading the
    news?
    Telegraph, telephone, and tell a girl.

19 Why should a group of pretty girls squeezing wet
    clothes remind us of going to church?
    Because the belles (bells) are wringing (ringing).

20   **Why do girls make good post-office clerks?**
Because they know how to manage the mails (males).

21   **Why should girls not learn French?**
Because one tongue is enough for any girl.

22   **Which is the favorite word with girls?**
The last one.

23   **Why are some girls like facts?**
Because they are stubborn things.

24   **Why are some girls like salad?**
Because they need a lot of dressing.

25   **Why is a bright girl's thought like the telegraph?**
Because it's so much quicker than the mail (male) intelligence.

26   **If there were only three girls in the world, what do you think they would talk about?**
Two of them would get together and talk about the other one.

27   **Why are some girls very much like teakettles?**
Because they sing away pleasantly and then all at once boil over.

28   **What is the difference between a girl and a parasol?**
You can shut up the parasol.

29   **When is a girl not a girl?**
When she is a bell (belle) or a deer (dear).

30   **What is the best way to find a mysterious girl out?**
Go around to her house when she isn't in.

31   **Why do girls like sunset and twilight so much?**
Because they are daughters of Eve.

32   **Why is a melancholy girl the most pleasant of all companions?**
Because she is always a-musing (amusing).

33 Why is a fashionable school for girls like a flower garden?
Because it's a place of haughty culture (horticulture).

34 Why should girls always set a good example?
Because boys are so apt to follow them.

35 When is a girl's cheek not a cheek?
When it's a little pail (pale).

36 Why are girls so extravagant about their clothes?
Because when they get a new dress, they wear it out the first day.

37 When is a girl not sorry to lose her hair?
When she has it cut.

38 Why are girls like umbrellas?
Because they are made out of ribs; you have to dress them in silk to make them look their best; at the least bit of a storm they go right up in the air; it is often your best friend who takes them away from you; and they are accustomed to reign (rain).

WHERE IN THE WORLD?

1 Where are the largest diamonds in New York City kept?
In the baseball fields.

2 Where are the kings of England usually crowned?
On the head.

3 Where can everyone always find money when he looks for it?
In the dictionary.

4 Where will you find the center of gravity?
At the letter V.

5 Where is the best place to get fat?
At the butcher shop.

6 Where did Noah strike the first nail he put in the ark?
On the head.

7 Where is the best place to have a very painful boil?
On someone else.

8 Where do you have the longest view in the world?
By a roadside where there are telephone poles, because there you can see from pole to pole.

1 If a father gives fifteen cents to his son and a dime to his daughter, what time of day is it?
A quarter to two.

2 If a pencil and a piece of paper had a race, which would win?
The pencil, because the paper would always remain stationary (stationery).

3 If ten sparrows were on a roof and you shot one, how many would remain?
None, because they would all fly away.

4 If a chicken could talk, what kind of language would it speak?
Foul (fowl) language, I'm afraid.

5 If your uncle's sister is not your aunt, just what relation is she to you?
She is your mother.

6 If you saw a counterfeit dollar bill on the sidewalk and walked by without picking it up, why should you be arrested?
Because you passed counterfeit money.

7   If a pretty girl wanted her father to take her rowing on a lake, what person in Greek mythology would she name?
    Europa (You row, pa).

8   If butter is fifty cents a pound in Chicago, what are window panes in Detroit?
    Glass.

9   If you add a syllable to a certain word it becomes shorter. What is the word?
    Short.

10 If you add to it, it becomes smaller. If you don't add to it, it becomes larger. What is it?
    A hole in your stocking. If you add thread to it, it becomes smaller.

11 If I were in the sun and you were out of it, what would the sun become?
    Sin.

12 If a man can mow a lawn a hundred feet square in two hours, how long will it take him to mow a lawn fifty feet square, if he mows at the same rate of speed?
    Half an hour. The second lawn is one-quarter as big as the first one.

13 If a two-wheeled conveyance is a bicycle, and a three-wheeled conveyance is a tricycle, what is a five-wheeled conveyance?
    A V-hicle.

14 If an acrobat fell off his trapeze, what would he fall against?
    Against his inclination.

15 If a boy wears his pants out, what will he do next?
    Wear them in again.

16   If a burglar got into the cellar, would the coal shoot
      (chute)?
      No, but the kindling would (wood).

17   If a little chicken could speak, and found an orange
      in its nest, what do you think it would say?
      Oh, look at the orange marmalade (mama laid).

18   If a man gets up on a donkey, where do you think he
      should get down?
      From a goose.

19   If you were invited out to dinner, and found nothing
      on the table but a beet, what would you say?
      Well, that beets all!

20   If the eyes and nose of a boy with a cold were to run
      a race, which would win?
      The eyes, for the nose would be blown, while the eyes
      would run till they dropped.

21   If a man tries to jump across a ditch and falls, why
      is he likely to miss seeing the beauties of summer?
      Because the Fall follows right after the Spring.

22   If a church should catch on fire, what part could not
      be saved?
      The organ, because the hose couldn't play on it.

23   If you were fishing in a harbor and a hostile warship
      came into sight, what would be the best thing to do?
      Pull up your line and sinker (sink her).

24   If a man shot at two frogs and killed one, what do
      you think the other frog would do?
      Croak.

25   If a goat should swallow a rabbit, what would be the
      result?
      A hare (hair) in the butter.

26 If a biscuit is a soda cracker, what is an ice pick?
A water cracker.

27 If one man carries a sack of flour and another man carries two sacks, which has the heavier load?
The one with a sack of flour, because a sack of flour is heavier than two (empty) sacks.

28 If I walk into a room full of people and put a new penny on the table in full view of everybody, what does the penny do?
It looks 'round.

29 If you lose a dollar today, why would it be a good plan to lose another tomorrow?
So as to make your loss a gain (again).

30 If a general should ask in vain for some martial music, what word would express his feelings?
Conundrum (Can none drum)?

31 If I were to bite off the end of your nose, what would the magistrate compel me to do?
Keep the peace (piece).

32 If Dick's father is Tom's son, what relation is Dick to Tom?
Tom is Dick's grandfather.

33 If you call a sheep's tail a leg, how many legs will he have?
He'll still have only four.

34 If a dog should lose his tail, where could he get another?
In a department store, where everything is retailed.

35 If a thief were engaged to sing in a chorus, what part would be most suitable for him?
The base (bass) part.

36 If you throw a white stone into the Red Sea, what will it become?
It will become wet.

37 If two postal telegraph operators were married in San Francisco, what would they make?
A Western Union.

38 If a postmaster went to the circus and a lion ate him, what time would it be?
Eight (ate) P.M.

39 If a tree were to break the panes of a window, what would the window panes say?
Tree, mend us (tremendous)!

40 If a farmer can raise two hundred bushels of corn in dry weather, what can he raise in wet weather?
An umbrella.

41 If you saw a bird sitting on a twig and you wanted to get the twig without disturbing the bird, what would you do?
Wait until the bird flew away.

42 If a man sent his son to college and paid a thousand dollars a year to put him through, how much change might he get back?
He might get a quarterback.

43 If a man smashed a clock, could he be accused of killing time?
Not if the clock struck first.

44 If you had a box of candles and no matches, how would you light them?
Just take one candle out of the box and then it will be a candle-lighter.

45 If one horse is shut up in a paddock and one is run-

ning loose down the road, which horse is singing, "Don't fence me in"?
Neither horse. Horses can't sing.

46   If you were locked in a room that had in it only a bed and a calendar, what would you do for food?
Get water from the bed springs and dates from the calendar.

47   If your neighbor quarreled with you and called you an insect, would he be wrong?
Yes, an insect has six legs.

48   If two is company, and three is a crowd, what are four and five?
Nine.

49   If I had an apple and you had only a bite, what would you do?
Scratch the bite.

50   If twelve makes a dozen, how many make a million?
Not very many.

GHOSTLY GUESSERS

If you lived in a graveyard:

1   With what would you open the gate?
    With a skeleton key.

2   What would you do if you got a bad cold that set-
    tled in your throat?
    Start coffin (coughin').

3   How would you identify in three letters a poem writ-
    ten for someone who had passed on?
    L-E-G (elegy).

4   What kind of jewels would you wear?
    Tombstones.

5   What would you do if you were getting ready for a
    play?
    Rehearse.

6   What would protect you from the sun?
    The shades.

7   Supposing a woman told you she was going to call?
    You would 'specter (expect her).

8   What would be your disposition?
    Grave.

HORSE LAUGHS

1   **How can you make a slow horse fast?**
Don't give him anything to eat for a while.

2   **How can you put a good horse on his mettle?**
Shoe him. That will put him on his metal.

3   **Barnum, the great circus man, had in his museum ten horses that had only twenty-four feet in all, yet they trotted about as well as other horses. How was this possible?**
The ten horses had twenty fore-feet.

4   **Why is a horse the most unusual feeder of all the animals?**
Because he eats best when there isn't a bit in his mouth.

5   **Why is a horse like the letter O?**
Because Gee (G) makes it GO.

6   **Why is a wild young horse like an egg?**
It must be broken before it can be used.

7   **Why are horses such great gossips?**
Because they are always tale bearers.

8   **Why is a well-trained horse like a kindhearted man?**
Because he always stops at the sound of whoa (woe).

9   **Why does tying a slow horse to a post make him a better racer?**
Because it makes him fast.

10   **What do you think is the principal part of a horse?**
His mane part.

11   **How can it be proved that a horse has six legs?**
Because he has forelegs (four legs) in front and two legs behind.

12   **Why is even a good-natured hunting horse likely to get angry unexpectedly?**
Because the better tempered he is, the easier he takes a fence (offense).

13   **What horse sees as much in the rear as he does in the front?**
A blind horse.

14   **What is wrong about describing a horse as a cart-horse?**
Because this description puts the cart before the horse.

WHAT'S THE DIFFERENCE?

1   What is the difference between an old penny and a new dime?
    Nine cents.

2   What is the difference between some people you know and a mirror?
    Some people you know talk without reflecting, while a mirror reflects without talking.

3   What is the difference between a cloud and a boy getting a spanking?
    The cloud pours with rain and the boy roars with pain.

4   What is the difference between a pianist and sixteen ounces of lead?
    The pianist pounds away and the lead weighs a pound.

5   What difference is there among a piano, a ship on a stormy sea, and you?
    The piano makes music. The ship makes you sick, and you make me sick. (Better be careful who you try this on!)

6   What is the difference between a naughty boy and a postage stamp?

You lick one with a stick, and you stick the other with a lick.

7   What is the difference between a cat and a comma?
    The cat has claws at the end of its paws, while the comma has its pause at the end of its clause.

8   What is the difference between a mouse and a beautiful girl?
    The mouse harms the cheese, and the girl charms the he's.

9   What is the difference between a man going to the second floor and a man looking upstairs?
    One is stepping upstairs, and the other is staring up steps.

10 What is the difference between an undersized witch and a deer trying to escape from a hunter?
    One is a stunted hag, and the other is a hunted stag.

11 What is the difference between a bottle of medicine and a bad boy?
    One is well shaken before taken, and the other should be taken and well shaken.

12 What is the difference between a moneyless man and a feather bed?
    One is hard up and the other is soft down.

13 What is the difference between a sailor and six broken clocks?
    The sailor goes to sea, and the clocks cease to go.

14 What is the difference between a man who has eaten a hearty meal and a man who has signed his will?
    One is dined and sated, and the other has signed and dated.

15 What is the difference between Christopher Columbus and the lid of a dish?
    One is a discoverer, and the other is a dish coverer.

16 What is the difference between a book of fiction and the rear light of a car?
One is a light tale, and the other is a tail light.

17 What is the difference between a glutton and a hungry man?
One eats too long, and the other longs to eat.

18 What is the difference between a china shop and a furniture store?
One sells tea sets, while the other sells settees.

19 What is the difference between a crazy hare and a counterfeit coin?
One is a mad bunny, and the other is bad money.

20 What is the difference between a barber and a woman with a lot of children?
One has razors to shave, and the other has shavers to raise.

21 What is the difference between an organist and a cold in the head?
One knows the stops, and the other stops the nose.

22 What is the difference between a book and a talkative bore?
You can shut up the book.

23 What is the difference between a man taking an oath of office and a suit of cast-off clothes?
One is sworn in, and the other is worn out.

24 What is the difference between a tailor and a groom?
One mends a tear, and the other tends a mare.

25 What is the difference between a weather forecaster and a watch key?
One watches the wind, while the other winds the watch.

26 What is the difference between a milkmaid and a sea-gull?
One skims milk, and the other skims water.

27 What is the difference between a postage stamp and a girl?
One is a mail fee, and the other is a female.

28 What is the difference between one yard and two yards?
Usually a fence.

29 What is the difference between a fisherman and a lazy schoolboy?
One baits his hook, while the other hates his book.

30 What is the difference between a person who is late for a train and a teacher in a girls' school?
One misses the train, and the other trains the misses.

31 What difference is there among a gardener, a billiard player, a precise man, and a church janitor?
The gardener minds his peas; the billiard player, his cues; the precise man, his p's and q's; and the church janitor, his keys and pews.

32 What is the difference between a beached ship and an airplane?
One grounds on the land, and the other lands on the ground.

33 What is the difference between a man struck with amazement and a leopard's tail?
One is rooted to the spot, while the other is spotted to the root.

34 What is the difference between an auction sale and seasickness?
One is a sale of effects, and the other, the effects of a sail.

35   What is the difference between a baby and a ship-wrecked sailor?
One clings to his ma, and the other clings to his spar (his pa).

36   What is the difference between a bee and a donkey?
One gets all the honey, and the other gets all the whacks (wax).

37   What is the difference between a piece of honeycomb and a black eye?
One is produced by a laboring bee, and the other by a be-laboring.

38   What is the difference between a bell and an organ?
One rings when it is told (tolled), but the other will be blowed first.

39   What is the difference between a blind man and a disabled sailor?
One can't see to go, and the other can't go to sea.

40   What is the difference between a millionaire and a prizefighter?
One makes money hand over fist, and the other makes his fist hand over money.

41   What is the difference between a prizefighter and a man with a cold?
One knows his blows, and the other blows his nose.

42   What is the difference between a boy who is twelve years old and a man taking a nap?
One is twelve, and the other is a-dozin' (dozen).

43   What is the difference between a school boy studying his lessons and a farmer watching his cows?
One is stocking his mind, and the other is minding his stock.

44   What is the difference between an elephant and a flea?
An elephant can have fleas, but a flea can't have elephants.

45   What is the difference between a jug of water and a man throwing his wife into the river?
One is water in the pitcher, and the other is pitch her in the water.

46   What is the difference between a chicken who can't hold up his head and seven days?
One is a weak one, and the other is one week.

47   What is the difference between an oak tree and a tight shoe?
One makes acorns, and the other makes corns ache.

48   What is the difference between a light in a cave and a dance in an inn?
One is a taper in a cavern, and the other is a caper in a tavern.

49   What difference is there among a rooster, Uncle Sam, and an old maid?
The rooster says "Cock-a-doodle-doo"; Uncle Sam says "Yankee Doodle Doo"; and the old maid says "Any dude'll do."

50   What is the difference between a locomotive engineer and a schoolteacher?
One minds the train, while the other trains the mind.

51   What is the difference between a farmer and a seamstress?
One gathers what he sows, and the other sews what she gathers.

52   What is the difference between a new sponge and a fashionably dressed man?

If you wet one it makes it swell, but if you wet the other it takes all the swell out of him.

53 **What is the difference between a hill and a pill?**
One is hard to get up, while the other is hard to get down.

54 **What is the difference between a hunting dog and a locomotive?**
One is trained to run, and the other runs a train.

55 **What is the difference between a man with an unnatural voice and one with unnatural teeth?**
One has a falsetto voice, and the other has a false set-o'-teeth.

56 **What is the difference between a professional violinist and the person who goes to hear him?**
One plays for his pay, and the other pays for his play.

57 **What is the difference between perseverance and obstinacy?**
One arises from a strong "will," and the other from a strong "won't."

58 **What is the difference between photographers and the whooping cough?**
One makes facsimiles and the other makes sick families.

59 **What is the difference between a church bell and a pickpocket?**
One peals from the steeple, and the other steals from the people.

60 **What is the difference among a king's son, a monkey's mother, a bald head, and an orphan?**
A king's son is an heir apparent, a monkey's mother is a hairy parent, a bald head has no hair apparent, and an orphan has nary a parent.

61   What is the difference between the Milky Way and a room full of great-grandfathers?

One is a lot of pale stars, and the other is a lot of stale pas.

62   What is the difference between a bright boy in school and shoe polish?

One shines at the head of the class, and the other shines at the foot.

63   What is the difference between a skilled marksman and the man who tends the targets?

One hits the mark, and the other marks the hits.

64   What is the difference between a grocer selling a pound of sugar and a druggist with a pestle and mortar?

One weighs a pound, and the other pounds away.

65   What is the difference between reckless speculation and some slices of bacon?

One is rash, and the other is a rasher.

66   What is the difference between the rising and the setting sun?

All the difference in the world.

67   What is the difference between the sun and bread?

The sun rises in the east, and the bread rises with the (y)east in it.

68   What is the difference between the manager of a theater and a sailor?

A sailor likes to see a lighthouse and the manager doesn't.

69   What is the difference between truth and eggs?

Truth crushed to earth will rise again, but eggs won't.

70   What is the difference between an honest and a dishonest laundress?

One irons your clothes, and the other steels (steals) them.

71 What is the difference between the land and the ocean?
One is dirt-y, and the other is tidy (tide-y).

72 What is the difference between a man and a banana peel?
Sometimes a man throws a banana peel in the gutter, and sometimes a banana peel throws a man in the gutter.

73 What is the difference between here and there?
The letter T.

ENIGMAS

Enigmas are riddles, often in verse form, in which there is a hidden meaning imaginatively described.

1   I'm not in earth, nor the sun, nor the moon.
    You may search all the sky—I'm not there.
    In the morning and evening—though not in the
        noon—
    You may plainly perceive me, for, like a balloon,
    I am midway suspended in air.
    Though disease may possess me, and sickness and
        pain,
    I am never in sorrow nor gloom;
    Though in wit and in wisdom
    I equally reign,
    I'm the heart of all sin and have long lived in vain;
    Yet I ne'er shall be found in the tomb.

The letter I.
(This is a famous enigma written by Lord Byron.)

2   Pray tell me, ladies, if you can,
    Who is that highly favored man,
    Who, though he has married many a wife,
    May still live single all his life?

A clergyman.

3   My first is in pork, but not in ham;
       My second in oyster, but not in clam;
       My third is in pond, but not in lake;
       My fourth is in hand, but not in shake;
       My fifth is in eye, but not in pink;
       My whole is a flower, you'll guess if you think.

Peony.

4   The beginning of eternity,
       The end of time and space,
       The beginning of every end,
       The end of every place.

The letter E.

5   Two hands I have and strange as it may be,
       I can be found in every big army.
       I'm always still except when roughly used,
       But I can be noisy when beat or abused.
       Soldiers of all nations rely on me,
       So I can be useful, as you can see.

A drum.

6   A headless man had a letter to write;
       It was read by one who had no sight;
       The dumb repeated it word for word,
       And he that was deaf both listened and heard.
       What was written?

The letter O, or nothing.

7   I am a caller at every home that you may meet,
       For daily I make my way along each street;
       Take one letter from me and still you will see
       I'm the same as before, as I always will be;
       Take two letters from me, or three or four,

I'll still be the same as I was before.
In fact, I'll say that all my letters you may take,
Yet of me nothing else you'll make.

A postman.

We are familiar little creatures,
Each has different forms and features.
One of us in a glass is set,
Another you will find in jet;
A third you'll find if you look in tin,
A fourth, a beautiful box within;
And the fifth, if you pursue,
It will never fly from you.

The vowels—A, E, I, O and U.

9   Just equal are my head and tail,
My middle slender as can be,
Whether I stand on head or heel,
'Tis all the same to you or me.
But if my head should be cut off,
The matter's true, although 'tis strange,
My head and body, severed thus,
Immediately to nothing change.

The figure 8.

10   I have wings yet never fly,
I have sails yet never go,
I can't keep still if I try,
Yet forever stand just so.

A windmill.

11   I go but never stir,
I count but never write,

I measure and divide and, sir,
You'll find my measures right.
I run but never walk,
I strike but never wound,
I tell you much but never talk
In all my daily round.

A clock.

12   Three-fourths of me an act display,
Three-fourths a bed for man;
Three-fourths have legs that cannot stray,
Three-fourths have legs that can.
I have a back without a spine,
An arm without a bone is mine.

A coat. Three-fourths of its letters spell act, cot (the
bed with legs that cannot stray), and cat (with legs
that can).

1   **When does a boat show affection?**
    When it hugs the shore.

2   **When does the sun get the best of an argument with
    the dew?**
    When it makes it dry up.

3   **When does a chair dislike you?**
    When it is broken and can't bear you.

4   **When does a farmer have the best chance to see his
    pigs?**
    When he has a sty on his eye.

5   **When is a door not a door?**
    When it is a jar (ajar).

6   **When is a lady not a lady?**
    When she turns into a drug store.

7   **When does a leopard change his spots?**
    When he moves.

8   **When does a man never fail to keep his word?**
    When no one will take it.

9   **When the clock strikes thirteen, what time is it?**
    Time to have the clock fixed.

10   **When is an artist very unhappy?**
When he draws a long face.

11   **When is a trunk emotional?**
When it is empty and easily moved.

12   **When is a doctor like an angry man?**
When he loses his patience (patients).

13   **When is it a good time for everyone to lose his temper?**
When it becomes bad.

14   **When is a blow on the head like a piece of fabric?**
When it is felt.

15   **When is a department store like a boat?**
When it has sales (sails).

16   **When is a bill like an old chair that is repaired?**
When it is receipted (re-seated).

17   **When is roast beef highest in price?**
When it is rarest.

18   **When do 2 and 2 make more than 4?**
When they make 22.

19   **When does a brave heart turn to stone?**
When it becomes a little bolder (boulder).

20   **When is a hat not a hat?**
When it becomes a girl.

21   **When is a man like a pony?**
When he is a little hoarse (horse).

22   **When is a chair like a kind of material?**
When it is sat in (satin).

23 **When is a man in love like a tailor?**
When he is pressing his suit.

24 **When is a soldier not a complete soldier?**
When he is in quarters.

25 **When is a ship at sea not on water?**
When it is on fire.

26 **When is a man where he never is and never could be?**
When he is beside himself.

27 **When a boy falls into the water, what is the first thing he does?**
Gets wet.

28 **When is money damp?**
When it's due (dew) in the morning and it's missed (mist) at night.

29 **When is a window like a star?**
When it is a skylight.

30 **When are two apples alike?**
When they are paired (pared).

31 **When is a baby like a china cup?**
When it's a-teething (a tea thing).

32 **When is a bald-headed man most likely to be reminded of his youth?**
When he thinks of his top.

33 **When is a boat like a heap of snow?**
When it's adrift (a drift).

34 **When do broken bones begin to make themselves useful?**
When they begin to knit.

35 **When are houses like books?**
When they have stories in them.

36 **When is a boy not a boy?**
When he's a bed (abed).

37 **When does a candle get angry?**
When it is put out or when it flares up.

38 **When was beef the highest it has ever been?**
When the cow jumped over the moon.

39 **When does a cow change places with her keeper?**
When she bellows, because then she is a cowherd
(cow heard).

40 **When is a chair treated most spitefully?**
When you have it caned simply because it can't bear
you.

41 **When is a chicken's neck like a bell?**
When it's rung (wrung) for dinner.

42 **When is a man both hospitable and a cheat at the
same time?**
When he takes you in.

43 **When is a chicken a glutton?**
When he takes a peck at a time.

44 **When is a clock on the stairs dangerous?**
When it runs down and strikes one.

45 **When can your coat pocket be empty and yet have
something in it?**
When it has a hole in it.

46 **When is coffee like the surface of the earth?**
When it is ground.

47   **When has a man the right to scold his coffee?**
When he has more than sufficient grounds.

48   **When are cooks most cruel?**
When they beat the eggs and whip the cream.

49   **When does a cook break the game laws?**
When she poaches some eggs.

50   **When is corn like a question?**
When you are popping it.

51   **When a man complains that his coffee is cold, what does his wife do?**
She makes it hot for him.

52   **When is an elevator not an elevator?**
When it is going down.

53   **When does a man shave himself with copper?**
When he cuts off his hair (heir) with a penny.

54   **When are eyes not eyes?**
When the wind makes them water.

55   **When a lady faints, what number will restore her?**
You must bring her 2.

56   **When does a farmer perform miracles?**
When he turns his horse to grass and turns his cows to pasture.

57   **When does a farmer act with cruelty to his corn?**
When he pulls its ears.

58   **When is a woman dressed like an Indian war chief in all his feathers?**
When she is dressed to kill.

59   **When are you most nearly related to a fish?**
When your grandmother is a dear old soul (sole).

60   **When are oysters like fretful people?**
When they're in a stew.

61   **When is a fruit stalk like a strong swimmer?**
When it stems the currants (currents).

62   **When is an apple not an apple?**
When it's a crab.

63   **When can you be said to have four hands?**
When you double your fists.

64   **When is your hair like a stick of wood?**
When it's knotted.

65   **When is a man like frozen rain?**
When he is hail (hale).

66   **When is a bright idea like a clock?**
When it strikes one.

67   **When is a girl's arm not an arm?**
When it's a little bare (bear).

68   **When is a lawyer like a crow?**
When he wishes his cause (caws) to be heard and gets
raving (raven) mad about it.

69   **When does a ship tell a falsehood?**
When she lies at the wharf.

70   **When did the lobster blush?**
When it saw the salad dressing.

71   **When is music like an icy pavement?**
When you will B flat if you don't C sharp.

72   **When is music like vegetables?**
When there are two beats (beets) to a measure.

73 **When is a nose not a nose?**
When it is a little radish (reddish).

74 **When is the water in the ocean most likely to escape?**
When it's only half-tied (half-tide).

75 **When can you say that a public speaker is a thief of lumber?**
When he takes the floor.

76 **When is a plant like a pig?**
When it begins to root.

77 **When does the hotel boy become a porter?**
When he reaches the lugg-age.

78 **When does a joke become a father?**
When the catch line becomes apparent (a parent).

79 **When does the rain become too familiar to a lady?**
When it begins to pat her (patter) on the back.

80 **When is a rope like a boy at school?**
When it is taut (taught).

81 **When is a piece of wood like a queen?**
When it is made into a ruler.

82 **When is a schoolboy like a postage stamp?**
When he is licked and put in a corner to make him stick to his letters.

83 **When is a sailor not a sailor?**
When he's a board (aboard).

84 **When is a ship in love?**
When she seeks a mate.

85 **When is a Scotchman like a donkey?**
When he strolls along his banks and braes (brays).

86 When a shoemaker is ready to make a shoe, what is the first thing he looks for?
The last.

87 When is a shoemaker like a doctor?
When he is heeling (healing).

88 When is silence likely to get wet?
When it reigns (rains).

89 When you go to a store for ten cents' worth of very sharp tacks, for what do you want them?
For ten cents.

90 When is a sick man a contradiction?
When he is an impatient patient.

91 When are you not yourself?
When you are a little pale (pail).

92 When does a man sneeze seven times?
When he can't help it.

93 When a small boy gets his stockings on wrong side out, what surprising thing does his mother do?
She turns the hose on him.

94 When are tailors and house agents both in the same business?
When they gather the rents.

95 When does a tailor serve his customers both well and ill?
When he gives them fits.

96 When do your teeth take over the functions of your tongue?
When they start to chatter.

97 When is a man greatly tickled but doesn't laugh?
When a fly lights on his nose.

98   When a tree is chopped down, why has it no reason
to complain?
Because it was axed (asked).

99   When is a trunk like two letters of the alphabet?
When it is empty (MT).

100   When are potatoes used for mending clothes?
When they are put in patches.

101   When is a loaded express wagon like a forest?
When it is full of trunks.

102   When is a wall like a fish?
When it is scaled.

103   When is it socially correct to serve milk in a saucer?
When you give it to a cat.

104   When is a restaurant like a woodshed?
When it is a chop-house.

105   When do elephants have eight feet?
When there are two of them.

106   When butter is worth twenty cents a pound, what
will a ton of coal come to?
Ashes.

107   When is a river like the letter T?
When it must be crossed.

108   When is the wind like a woodchopper?
When it is cutting.

109   When does an automobile go exactly as fast as a
train?
When it is on the train.

110   When may we say a student is very hungry?
When he devours his books.

111   **When does a bather capture a large bird?**
When he takes a duck in the water.

112   **When is an altered dress like a secret?**
When it is let out.

113   **When is a house like a crow?**
When it has wings.

114   **When is the time on a clock like the whistle on a train?**
When it's two to two (toot-toot-too).

115   **When you look around you on a cold winter morning, what do you see on every hand?**
A glove.

116   **When should any pig be able to write?**
When he has been turned into a pen.

117   **When is a piece of string like a stick of wood?**
When it has knots in it.

118   **When is a horse like a house?**
When it has blinds on.

1   **What country suggests a straw hat?**
Panama.

2   **What country expresses anger?**
Ireland.

3   **What country mourns?**
Wales.

4   **What country has a good appetite?**
Hungary.

5   **What country is popular on Thanksgiving Day?**
Turkey.

6   **What country is a coin?**
Guinea.

7   **What country does the cook use?**
Greece.

8   **What country is good for skaters?**
Iceland.

9   **What country is useful at mealtime?**
China.

BIBLE RIDDLES

1 **When were automobiles mentioned in the Bible?**
When Elijah went up on high.

2 **Who was the most successful doctor in the Bible?**
Job, because he had the most patients (patience).

3 **Who was the most popular actor in the Bible?**
Samson. He brought down the house.

4 **When is money first mentioned in the Bible?**
When the dove brought the "green" back to the ark.

5 **When is high finance first mentioned in the Bible?**
When Pharaoh's daughter took a little profit (prophet) from the bulrushes.

6 **At what time of day was Adam created?**
A little before Eve.

7 **When was radio first mentioned in the Bible?**
When the Lord took a rib from Adam and made it into a loud speaker (Eve).

8 **What evidence does the Bible give to show that Adam and Eve were rather noisy?**
They raised Cain.

9   **Why couldn't Eve have the measles?**
Because she'd Adam (had 'em).

10   **What animal took the most baggage into the ark, and what animals the least?**
The elephant took his trunk, but the fox and the rooster took only a brush and a comb between them.

11   **What did the cat say when the ark landed?**
Is that Ararat?

12   **What simple affliction caused the death of Samson?**
He died of fallen arches.

13   **Who was the best financier in the Bible?**
Noah. He floated his stock (animals) while the whole world was in liquidation.

14   **What man in the Bible had no parents?**
Joshua, the son of Nun.

15   **Why should we be encouraged by the story of Jonah and the whale?**
Because Jonah was down in the mouth, but came out all right.

16   **Who was the straightest man in the Bible?**
Joseph, because Pharaoh made a ruler out of him.

17   **Who is the smallest man mentioned in the Bible?**
Bildad, the Shuhite (shoe-height).

18   **Why was Lot's wife turned into a pillar of salt?**
Because she was dissatisfied with her Lot.

19   **What was it that Adam and Eve never had and yet they gave to their children?**
Parents.

20   **What was the longest day in the Bible?**
When there was no Eve in it.

21   Did Eve ever have a date with Adam?
No; it was an apple.

22   How long did Cain hate his brother?
As long as he was Abel.

23   Who in the Bible was the champion runner of all time?
Adam. He was the first in the human race.

24   What did the Egyptians do when it got dark?
They turned on the Israelites.

25   Who in the Bible was the first and the largest guardian of another person?
The whale. He brought up Jonah.

26   What did they use to do arithmetic with in Bible times?
The Lord told them to multiply on the face of the earth.

27   When was tennis first mentioned in the Bible?
When Joseph served in Pharaoh's court.

28   What was the first theatrical venture in the Bible?
When Eve appeared for Adam's benefit.

29   When was the first meat mentioned in the Bible?
Noah took Ham into the ark.

30   When was medicine first mentioned in the Bible?
When the Lord gave Moses two tablets.

31   What was the first gift mentioned in the Bible?
Eve presented Adam with a cane (Cain).

32   Why did Adam bite the apple?
Because he didn't have a knife.

33   **How do we know that Noah was preceded from the ark by at least three other people?**
Because the Bible says that Noah came forth (fourth).

34   **Why was the giant Goliath very much astonished when David hit him with a stone?**
Because such a thing had never before entered his head.

35   **What sentence of three words which reads the same backward and forward did Adam use when he introduced himself to Eve?**
"Madam, I'm Adam."

36   **Do you know about the baseball game in the Bible?**
Eve stole first; Adam stole second; Rebecca walked to the well with the pitcher; then Gideon rattled the pitchers; Goliath was put out by David; and the prodigal son made a home run.

37   **Why didn't Noah catch more fish than he did during the voyage of the ark?**
Because he had only two worms.

38   **How were the Egyptians paid for the goods taken by the Israelites when they fled from Egypt?**
The Egyptians received a check on the Bank of the Red Sea.

39   **Where was Noah when the light went out?**
In d-ark.

40   **How was Ruth rude to Boaz?**
She pulled his ears and trod on his corn.

41   **Who was the strongest man in the Bible?**
Jonah, because the whale couldn't hold him even after he got him down.

42   **What proof have we that there was sewing in the time of David?**
He was hemmed in on all sides.

8   Why is the history of England like a wet season?
Because it is so full of rains (reigns).

9   When could the British Empire be purchased for the smallest amount?
When King Richard III offered his kingdom for a horse.

SECRETS OF THE SEAS

1   What is the most insurgent sea?
2   What is a sea that is good and safe?
3   What is the calmest sea?
4   What is a very old sea?
5   What sea shows an orderly sequence of events?
6   What sea is always prim and precise?
7   What sea adds a nice flavor to food?
8   What sea is it that has nearly finished its schooling?
9   What sea is it that breaks away?
10 What sea is very choosy?
11 What sea shuts itself apart from the world?
12 What sea follows as a result of something that has
    gone before?
13 What sea is very harsh and stern?

1 Sedition 2 Security 3 Serenity 4 Senility 5 Series
6 Sedate 7 Seasoning 8 Senior 9 Secession 10 Se-
lectivity 11 Seclusion 12 Sequence 13 Severity

1   Sam Patch always goes up to the tallest trees, takes
     off his boots and jumps over them. How can this be?
     He just jumps over his boots.

2   Down South, it is said, the mosquitoes are so large
     that a good many of them weigh a pound, and they
     sit on the logs and bark when people go by. How
     can this be?
     A good many of them taken together would weigh
     a pound, and they sit on the bark (of trees).

3   A doctor had a brother who went out West. But the
     man who went out West had no brother. How can
     this be?
     The doctor was a lady doctor.

4   Two men, with their two wives and two sons, are relat-
     ed to each other as follows: The men are each other's
     fathers and sons, their wives' fathers and husbands,
     and their children's fathers and grandfathers. The
     women are the children's mothers and sisters; and the
     boys are uncles to each other. How can this be?
     The two men had been widowers, and married each
     other's daughters.

5   A train ran off a big bridge recently and no one was killed or injured. How can this be?

It ran off the bridge at one end as usual and went on its way along the tracks.

6   Three men are under an umbrella, but none of them gets wet. How can this be?

It isn't raining.

7   There was a carpenter who made a cupboard door which proved to be too big. He cut it, and unfortunately then he cut it too little. He thereupon cut it again and made it fit beautifully. How can this be?

He didn't cut it enough the first time. He cut it too little.

8   The schoolteacher and his daughter, the minister's wife and the minister, are out walking in the woods. They find a bird's nest with four eggs in it. Each of them takes out an egg and yet one egg is left in the nest. How can this be?

There were only three people, because the minister's wife was the schoolteacher's daughter.

ANIMAL
CRACKERS

1 What animal are you when you have a cold?
   Horse.

2 What animals are in all banks?
   Doe and bucks.

3 What animal is on every legal document?
   A seal.

4 What animal is in every baseball game?
   A bat. (Yes, a bat is an animal.)

5 What animal needs clothing, poor thing?
   Bear (bare).

6 What animal never plays fair?
   Cheetah (cheater).

7 What animal is nearest to your brain?
   Hare (hair).

8 What animal do you need when you are driving a
   car?
   A good steer.

9 What animal is your girl-friend?
   Deer.

10   What animal is tiresomely talkative?
      Boar.

11   What animal has the most brains of any?
      A hog, because he has a hogshead full of them.

12   Why is the camel so easily angered?
      Because he always has his back up.

13   When is a donkey spelled with one letter?
      When it's U, dear.

14   What two animals go with you everywhere?
      Your calves.

15   What animals do you find in the clouds?
      Reindeer (rain, dear).

16   What animal would you like to be on a very cold
      day?
      A little otter (hotter).

17   What farm animal is very much like a cannibal?
      A cow, because it always wants to eat its fodder
      (father).

18   Which animal is the heaviest in all creation?
      A led (lead) horse.

19   What well-known animal drives an automobile?
      A road hog.

WHAT IS IT?

1   What is it that has eyes but can't see?
A potato.

2   What is it that grows larger the more you take away
from it?
A hole.

3   What is it that everybody gives but few take?
Advice.

4   What is it that is always behind time?
The back of a watch.

5   What is it that passes in front of the sun yet casts no
shadow?
The wind.

6   What is it that is bought by the yard but worn by the
foot?
A carpet.

7   As I was going through the woods, I found something, picked it up and couldn't find it, ran home,
looked for it, found it, didn't want it and threw it
away. What was it?
A thorn in my foot.

8   What is it that is black and white and red all over?
A book.

9   What is it that has a tongue but cannot talk?
A shoe.

10   What valuable thing that he never had and never will
have does a man give a woman?
A husband.

11   What is it that has legs but can't walk?
A table or a chair.

12   What is it that lives in winter, dies in summer, and
grows with its roots upward?
An icicle.

13   What is it that contains more feet in winter than in
summer?
An outdoor skating rink.

14   What is it that you ought to keep after you have
given it to someone else?
A promise.

15   What is it that can and does speak in every known
language and yet never went to school?
An echo.

16   What is it that will go up a chimney down, but won't
go down the chimney up?
An umbrella.

17   What is it that goes all the way from New York to
San Francisco without moving an inch?
The road.

18   What is it that everyone in the world is doing at the
same time?
Growing older.

19   What is it that is always cracked when it is heard?
      A joke.

20   What is it that has two heads, six feet, one tail and
      four ears?
      A man on horseback.

21   What is it that goes farther the slower it goes?
      Your money.

22   What is it that may be lost yet at the same time its
      location may be known?
      A needle in a haystack.

23   What is it that never has anything to say, but its ac-
      tion is always directly to the point?
      A wasp.

24   What is it that everyone has to catch before he can
      sing?
      His breath.

25   What is it that though dark has done most to en-
      lighten the world?
      Ink.

26   What is it that is alive and has only one foot?
      A leg.

27   What is it that is always coming but never arrives?
      Tomorrow. When it arrives, it is today.

28   What is it that can be broken without being hit or
      dropped?
      Silence.

29   What is it that you need most in the long run?
      Your breath.

30   What is it that gets less tired the farther it goes?
      An auto wheel.

31   What is it that everybody wants, and yet wants to get rid of as soon as possible?
A good appetite.

32   What is it that works when it plays and plays when it is working?
A fountain.

33   What is it that a man can be that a woman can't?
The father of a family.

34   What is it that always walks with its head downward?
A nail in your shoe.

35   What is it that, while it is yours alone, is used much more by other people than by yourself?
Your name.

36   What is it that becomes too young the longer it exists?
A portrait of a person.

37   What is it that is often given to you, but which you never have, and yet often have to give up?
A conundrum.

38   What is it that goes around the house in daytime and lies in a corner at night?
A broom.

39   What is it that we never borrow but often return?
Thanks.

40   What is it that grows longer the more it is cut?
A ditch.

41   What is it we all say we will do, tell others to do, and yet no one has ever done it?
Stop a minute.

42 What is it that everyone can divide, but no one can see the place at which it has been divided?
Water.

43 What is it that, supposing its greatest length to be nine inches, width four inches, and depth three inches, still contains a solid foot?
A shoe.

44 What is it that has eight feet and can sing?
A quartet.

45 What is it that goes all day, comes in at night, and stands with its tongue out?
A wagon.

46 What is it that we have in December that we don't have in any other month?
The letter D.

47 What is it that goes up and never goes down?
Your age.

48 What is it that falls often but never gets hurt?
Snow.

49 What is it that has eighteen legs and catches flies?
A baseball team.

50 What is it that, when once lost, you can never find again?
Time.

51 What is it that stays hot in a refrigerator?
Mustard.

52 What is it that you cannot see, but is always before you?
The future.

WHY ARE THEY ALIKE?

1. **Why are authors and chickens alike?**
Because both have to scratch for a living.

2. **Why are a railroad engine and the family wash alike?**
Because both of them go on a line.

3. **Why are a bad boy and a dirty rug alike?**
Because both of them need a beating.

4. **Why are a bruise and a bubble alike?**
Because both are caused by a blow.

5. **Why are clouds and horseback riders alike?**
Because they both hold the rains (reins).

6. **Why is a vote in Congress like a cold?**
Because sometimes the ayes have it, and sometimes the noes.

7. **Why is the head chef of a big hotel like a man on top of the Washington Monument?**
Because they are both in a high culinary (high, cool and airy) situation.

8. **Why is a coward like a leaky faucet?**
Because both of them run.

9   **Why is a steel trap like the measles?**
Because it's catching.

10   **Why is a bad joke like an unsharpened pencil?**
Because it has no point.

11   **Why is a baseball umpire like a dog?**
Because he wears a muzzle, snaps at flies, and is always chasing fouls (fowls).

12   **Why are weathervanes like loafers?**
Because they both go around doing nothing.

13   **Why is a letter like a bottle of perfume?**
Because both are sent (scent).

14   **Why is a hat on the head like a bucket full of water?**
Because they are both filled to the brim.

15   **Why are a hobo and a balloon alike?**
Because both are without any visible means of support.

16   **Why are a river and a clock alike?**
Because neither of them runs without winding.

17   **Why are money and a secret alike?**
Because both of them are hard to keep.

18   **Why are talkative people and male pigs alike?**
Because after a while both of them become bores (boars).

19   **Why are the posts of a gate and vegetable seeds alike?**
Because they both prop-a-gate.

20   **Why is a mouse like hay?**
Because the cat'll (cattle) eat it.

21 Why is a good architect like a popular actor?
Because they both draw good houses.

22 Why is a defeated baseball team like wool?
Because it is worsted.

23 Why is a large tree like a trip around the world?
Because its root (route) is a long one.

24 Why is riding in an airplane like falling down stairs?
Because it makes you soar (sore).

25 Why are some children like flannel?
Because they shrink from washing.

26 Why is a sleepless person like a worn piece of cloth?
Because he has no nap.

27 Why are sticks of candy like horses?
Because the more you lick them the faster they go.

28 Why is a dog biting its tail like a good manager?
Because he is making both ends meet.

29 Why is bread like the sun?
Because it isn't light before it rises.

30 Why is an empty room like a room full of married people?
Because there isn't a single person in it.

31 Why is a bowl of flowers on a table like a speech made on the deck of a ship?
Because it is a decoration (deck oration).

32 Why is a bad cold like a great humiliation?
Because it brings the proudest man to his sneeze (his knees).

33 Why is a dilapidated house like old age?
Because its gate (gait) is feeble and its locks are few.

34   Why is a nail fast in the wall like an old man?
Because it is in firm (infirm).

35   Why is a person with rheumatism like a window?
Because he is full of pains (panes).

36   Why is greediness like a bad memory?
Because it is always forgetting (for getting).

37   Why are a blacksmith and a safe, gentle horse alike?
Because one is a horse-shoer and the other is a sure
horse.

38   Why is a duke like a book?
Because he has a title.

39   Why is a loaf of bread four weeks old like a mouse
running into a hole in the wall?
Because you can see its tail (it's stale).

40   Why is a cat going up three flights of stairs like a
high hill?
Because she's a-mountin' (a mountain).

41   Why is a plum pudding like the ocean?
Because it is full of currants (currents).

42   Why is a crash of thunder like a jeweler?
Because both make the ear ring.

43   Why is a baseball game like a pancake?
Because its success depends on the batter.

44   Why is a windy orator like a whale?
Because he often rises to spout.

45   Why is a healthy boy like the United States?
Because he has a good constitution.

CAN YOU
FIGURE
THESE
OUT?

1 **Why is the figure 9 like a peacock?**
Because without its tail it is nothing (0).

2 **What figure increases its value by one-half when turned upside down?**
The figure 6.

3 **Why is an account book like a model agency?**
Because it is full of figures.

4 **Why should the number 288 never be mentioned in polite company?**
Because it is too gross (two gross).

5 **Why is twice ten like two times eleven?**
Because twice ten is twenty, and two times eleven is twenty too (twenty-two).

6 **From what number can you take half and leave nothing?**
The number 8. Take away the top half and 0 is left.

7 **Add half a score to nothing and what animal does it make?**
O and X (10) added together make ox.

8   Add two figures to 19 and make it less than 20.
$19\frac{1}{2}$.

9   If a cork and a bottle cost $2.10, and the bottle costs
$2.00 more than the cork, what does the cork cost?
The cork costs $.05, and the bottle costs $2.05.

10   What is the difference between 100 and 1,000?
Nothing (0).

11   See if you can put three sixes together so as to make
seven.
6 6/6.

12   What fraction, if you turn it upside down, will have
exactly the same value as before you turned it upside
down?
6/9.

13   What is the difference between twice twenty-two and
twice two and twenty?
The first is 44, and the second is 24.

14   What two numbers multiplied together will give you
seven?
Few people ever seem to think of these two numbers.
They are 7 and 1.

15   Can you show that eight 8's added together add up
to 1,000?

```
       888
        88
         8
         8
         8
     ------
     1,000
```

16   Two women went shopping. One spent $10.00 more than the other, and together they spent $40.00. How much money did each of them spend?
One spent $15.00 and the other spent $25.00.

17   If you double a number between 1 and 10, the result will be the same as if you added 2 to it. What is the number?
2.

18   How many times can 19 be subtracted from 190?
Only once, because any later subtractions wouldn't be from 190, but from a smaller number.

19   What three figures multiplied by 4 give 5?
1.25 (1¼).

CATS!
CATS!
CATS!

1	What cat is fuzzy and looks like a worm?
2	What cat is a cat that flies?
3	What cat is a quiz cat?
4	What cat is a tree?
5	What cat is a wild cat?
6	What cat is a bad cat for the eyes?
7	What cat is a shooting cat?
8	What cat gives you a cold in the head?
9	What cat is a very calamitous cat?
10	What cat is a very violent and destructive cat?
11	What cat is a tool of a scheming person?
12	What cat is a rancher's cat?
13	What cat is a fisherman's cat?
14	What cat is found in a library?
15	What cat is a loud, harsh cry?
16	What cat is a violinist's cat?
17	What cat is a church cat?
18	What cat is a classification?
19	What cat is a waterfall?

1 Caterpillar 2 Catbird 3 Catechism 4 Catalpa
5 Catamount 6 Cataract 7 Catapult 8 Catarrh
9 Catastrophe 10 Cataclysm 11 Catspaw 12 Cattle
13 Catfish 14 Catalogue 15 Caterwaul 16 Catgut
17 Cathedral 18 Category 19 Cataract

1   What amount of money can be divided fifty-fifty be-
    tween two persons, giving one person a hundred
    times more than the other?
    Fifty dollars and fifty cents.

2   There is one thing that no one knows any more about
    no matter how much it is looked into. What is it?
    A mirror.

3   A tree, a horn, tongues and laces have to do with
    something we wear. What is it?
    Shoes.

4   A man bought two fishes and had three when he got
    home. How did this happen?
    He had two fishes—and one smelt.

5   On which side of a church does a yew tree grow?
    On the outside.

6   The first part of an odd number is removed and it
    becomes even. What number is it?
    (S)even.

7   At what time of life does everyone weigh the most?
    When he is the heaviest.

8   What two vegetables begin and end with the same two letters in the same order?
Tomato and onion.

9   Can you name eight different subjects taught in school or college that end in ics?
Economics, ethics, mathematics, physics, mechanics, dramatics, civics, calisthenics.

10   Soldiers mark time with their feet. What does the same thing with its hands?
A watch.

11   Sisters and brothers have I none, but that man's father is my father's son. Who am I looking at?
My own son.

12   What miracle happened when Mr. Stone and Mr. Wood stood on a corner and a pretty girl passed by?
Stone turned to Wood and Wood turned to Stone. Then they both turned to look. The girl turned into a beauty shop.

13   Suppose there was a cat in each corner of the room; a cat sitting opposite each cat; a cat looking at each cat; and a cat sitting on each cat's tail. How many cats would there be?
Four. Each cat was sitting on its own tail.

14   A girl had an aunt who was in love. She sent her an animal whose name urged the aunt to run away and get married. The aunt sent her back a fruit that brought the message that this was impossible. What was the animal and what was the fruit?
Antelope (aunt, elope) and canteloupe (can't elope).

15   What are two of the greatest modern miracles?
The deaf-mute who picked up a wheel and spoke, and the blind man who picked up a hammer and saw.

16   A duck, a frog and a skunk went to the circus. Each had to have a dollar to get in. Which got in, and which didn't?

The duck got in because she had a bill. The frog got in on his green-back. But the poor old skunk couldn't get in because he had only a cent (scent), and it was a bad one.

17   Abraham Lincoln was asked how long a man's legs should be to be the most serviceable. What was his answer?

Long enough to reach the ground.

18   Can you tell me of what parentage Napoleon I was?

Of course I can (of Corsican).

19   What is it that stands aloft and regulates our daily program, yet feels no interest in our concerns; directs us when to go and when to come, yet cares not about our actions; often strikes a heavy blow to urge us on, and we feel no resentment when this reproof is given?

A clock.

20   The king's fool offended him and was condemned to death. The king said: "You have been a good fool, so I will let you choose the manner of your death." What manner of death did the fool choose?

To die of old age.

21   How many eggs can a man eat on an empty stomach?

None. As soon as he begins to eat even one bite of an egg, his stomach is no longer empty.

22   On a clear winter's day, what are the best fishes to fasten together?

Skates, soles and (h)eels.

23   An old woman in a red cloak was crossing a field in which there was a goat. What strange transformation suddenly took place?

The goat turned to butter (butt her) and the old woman became a scarlet runner.

24 Speaking of milk, said the milk bottle, have you heard of the strange case of the Boston baby brought up on elephant's milk?
It was the elephant's baby.

25 Can you spell "blind pig" with two letters?
Pg (pig without an eye).

26 Do you know the difference between a bicycle and a sewing machine?
If you don't, you'd better be careful the next time you go to buy a bicycle, or they may sell you a sewing machine.

27 Tell me the name of the oldest whistler in the world, and what tune he whistled?
The wind, whistling "Over the hills and far away."

28 How can you tie a cross to a monkey and turn him into a point?
Add X to ape, and it becomes "apex."

29 Can you make sense out of the following:
Yy u r yy u b
I c u r yy 4 me.
Too wise you are, too wise you be,
I see you are too wise for me.

30 How can you divide seventeen apples absolutely equally among eleven small boys?
Make the apples into applesauce, and measure it out very carefully.

31 There were sixteen ears of corn in a barrel. A rabbit came each night and carried away three ears. How long did it take him to empty the barrel?
It took him sixteen nights, because each night he carried away one ear of corn and his own two ears. This made three ears each night.

32   Smith bet that he could eat more oysters than Jones. Smith ate ninety in a week, and Jones ate a hundred and one. How many more did Jones eat than Smith?
Ten. He ate a hundred and won.

33   There is a girl in a candy store in Denver who is 6 feet 6 inches tall, has a waist measure of 42 inches, and wears number 12 shoes. What do you think she weighs?
She weighs candy.

34   Write down VOLIX, and ask a friend how to pronounce it.
Volume nine (Vol. IX).

35   Mr. Brown said: "I could make a success in my business only by reversing the usual rule. I had to start at the top and work down." What is Mr. Brown's business?
He is a paperhanger.

36   How might you be completely sleepless for seven days and still not lack any rest?
By sleeping nights.

37   How can you make fifteen bushels of corn from one bushel?
By popping it.

38   How can you make sense out of the following sentence: "It was and I said not but"?
"It was AND, I said, not BUT."

39   If a carpenter receives twenty-five cents for sawing a board into two lengths, how much should he receive for sawing the board into four lengths?
Seventy-five cents, because it takes only three saw-cuts.

40   Each of the Flapdoodle brothers has as many sisters
     as he has brothers. But each of the Flapdoodle sisters
     has twice as many brothers as she has sisters. How
     many brothers and sisters are there in the Flapdoodle
     family?
     Four brothers and three sisters.

41   Can you make the following make sense:
     Stand   take   to   world
     I   you   throw   the
     I understand you undertake to overthrow the under-
     world.

42   Down on our farm we had a hen that laid an egg six
     inches long. Can you beat that?
     Yes, with an eggbeater.

43   Do you believe in clubs for young people?
     Only when kindness fails.

44   What relation is that child to its father who is not its
     father's own son?
     His daughter.

45   Name a carpenter's tool you can spell forward and
     backward the same way.
     Level.

46   "Railroad crossing,
     Look out for the cars";
     Can you spell it without any R's?
     I—t spells "it."

47   Two Indians are standing on a hill, and one is the
     father of the other's son. What relation are the two
     Indians to each other?
     Husband and wife.

WHO IN THE WORLD?

1 Who are the best acrobats in your house?
   The pitchers and the tumblers.

2 Who in Shakespeare's plays killed the greatest number of chickens?
   Hamlet's uncle, because he "did murder most foul."

3 Who are the best bookkeepers?
   The people who never return the books you lend them.

4 Who always has a number of movements on foot for making money?
   A dancing teacher.

5 Who handles more letters in a day than the busiest of Uncle Sam's postmen?
   A hard-working typesetter.

6 Who is a man who always finds things dull?
   A scissors grinder.

7 Who dares to sit before the Queen of England with his hat on?
   Her chauffeur.

8 Who always goes to bed with his shoes on?
   A horse.

CHARADE RIDDLES

Written charades are very much like those you act out when you play the game of charades at a party. The answer to each is a word, and the charade itself describes each syllable of the word. The word "charade" comes from the Spanish charrada, which means the speech of a clown. Charades are composed in both prose and verse. Here are some prose ones for you to try:

1   My first is company; my second is a veiled lady who shuns company; my third assembles company; and my whole amuses company.
    Co-nun-drum.

2   My first is a number; my second is found in the head; my third is what my second does; and my whole is an American state.
    Tennessee (ten-eye-see).

3   My first is something you should do; my second is an exclamation; my third is a great crowd of people; my fourth is a wormlike fish; and my whole is something you ride in.
    Automobile (ought-oh-mob-eel).

4   Without my first, my second could never have existed, and my whole is as old as creation.
    Sun-day.

5   My first is used in driving a horse; my second is needy; my third is a boy's name; and my whole is a bird.
Whip-poor-will.

6   My first means equality; my second inferiority; and my whole superiority.
Match-less.

7   My first is a pronoun; my second is used at weddings; and my whole is a fish.
Her-ring.

8   My first is a farm animal; my second is another animal. My second worried my first, and thus proved himself to be my whole.
Bull-dog.

9   My first is a vehicle; my second is a preposition; and my whole is a cozy part of a ship.
Cab-in.

10   My first is a kitchen utensil; my second is a big body of water; and my whole is a well-known flower.
Pansy (pan-sea).

11   My first is a vehicle; my second is what the United States is; and my whole is a flower.
Car-nation.

12   My first is a pronoun; my second is not high; my third we all must do; my fourth is a plural pronoun; and my whole is musical.
Melodious—me-low-die-us.

13   My first is found in every country of the globe; my second is what we all should be; and my whole is the same as my first.
Man-kind.

RHYMED CHARADES

1   My first some gladly take
     Entirely for my second's sake;
     But few, indeed, will ever care
     Both together ever to bear.
     Misfortune (Miss-fortune).

2   My first is a tool,
     My second a coin;
     My whole is speech that's sometimes annoying.
     Accent (Ax-cent).

3   My first is what you're doing now,
     My second is obtained from stone;
     Before my whole you often stand,
     But mostly when you're all alone.
     Looking-glass.

4   My first's an ugly insect,
     My second, an ugly brute;
     My whole's an ugly phantom,
     Which nought can please or suit.
     Bug-bear.

5   My first is what,
     My second is not,
     And my whole you put in a corner.
     A whatnot.

6   My number, definite and known,
Is ten times ten, told ten times o'er;
Though half of me is one alone,
And half exceeds all count and score.

Thou-sand.

7   My first of anything is half,
My second is complete;
And so remains until once more
My first and second meet.

Semi-circle.

8   My first I hope you are,
My second I see you are,
My whole I know you are.

Wel-come.

9   Without my first you'd look very strange,
My second we all want to be;
My whole is what many a lady has worn
At a dance or a party or tea.

Nose-gay.

10   My first is myself in a short little word,
My second's a plaything, and you are my third.

Idol (I-doll).

11   My first is a circle, my second a cross,
If you meet with my whole, look out for a toss.

Ox.

12   My first is a part of the day,
My last a conductor of light;
My whole to take measure of time
Is useful by day and by night.

Hour-glass.

HOW COME?

1   How many girls would it take, standing in single file, to reach from Fort Worth to Dallas, which is about thirty miles?
About thirty girls, because a miss is as good as a mile.

2   How far can you go into the woods?
As far as the middle. After that, you will be going out.

3   How can five people divide five cookies so that each gets a cookie and yet one cookie remains on the plate?
The last person takes the plate with the cookie.

4   How would you most easily swallow a door?
By bolting it.

5   How does the fireplace feel when you fill it with coal?
Grateful (grate full).

6   How can we know that a lion has whiskers?
Because he is so often bearded in his den.

7   How would you most easily increase the speed of a slow boat?
By making it fast to the dock.

8   **How can bookkeeping be taught in a lesson of three words?**
Never lend them.

9   **How can you keep a rooster from crowing on Sunday?**
By getting him stuffed on Saturday night.

10   **How can you make a thin child fat?**
Throw him into the air and he'll come down plump.

11   **How can you make a coat last?**
Make the trousers and vest first.

12   **How do we know that a dentist is unhappy in his work?**
Because he looks down in the mouth.

13   **How would you say in one word that you had just encountered a doctor?**
Met-a-physician.

14   **How do locomotives hear?**
Through their engineers (engine-ears).

15   **How can a place be lighted by a thousand fires, yet give no warmth, neither can we put them out?**
When it is lighted by fireflies.

16   **How many bushel baskets full of earth can you take out of a hole that is three feet square and three feet deep?**
None. The earth has already been taken out.

17   **How can you shoot one hundred and twenty hares at one shot?**
Fire at a wig.

18   **How can hunters best find their game in the woods?**
By listening to the bark of the trees.

19 **How can you best learn the value of money?**
    By trying to borrow some.

20 **How many of his relations live on a landlord's property?**
    His ten aunts (tenants).

21 **How can you always have what you please?**
    By always being pleased with what you have.

22 **How does a boy feel who has been kept after school for bad spelling?**
    Simply spell-bound.

23 **How would you speak of a tailor when you couldn't remember his name?**
    As Mr. So-and-so (Sew-and-sew).

24 **How can you make a tall man short?**
    By borrowing a lot of money from him.

25 **How can a man with false teeth have a new set of teeth inserted free of charge?**
    By kicking a bulldog. The bulldog will quickly insert his teeth.

26 **How can you change a pumpkin into a squash?**
    Throw it up high and it will come down a squash.

27 **How long will an eight-day clock run without winding?**
    It won't run at all without winding.

28 **How is it possible to get up late in the day and yet rise when the rays of the sun first come through the window?**
    By sleeping in a bedroom facing the west.

29 **How does a sailor know there is a man in the moon?**
    Because he has been to see (sea).

MISS TREES
(MYSTERIES)

1   What tree does everyone carry in his hand?
Palm.

2   What tree is a kind of grasshopper?
Locust.

3   What tree is an inlet of the sea?
Bay.

4   What tree is like an old joke?
Chestnut.

5   What tree is always very sad?
Weeping willow.

6   What tree is a good-looking girl?
Peach.

7   What tree is a carpenter's tool?
Plane.

8   What tree grows at the seaside?
Beech.

9   What is the most important of all the trees in history?
Date.

10   **What tree always has a neat appearance?**
Spruce.

11   **What tree goes into ladies' winter coats?**
Fir (fur).

12   **What tree is always longing for someone?**
Pine.

13   **What tree is one of your parents?**
Pawpaw (Papa).

14   **What trees are nice to kiss?**
Tulip (trees).

15   **What tree is always in high favor?**
Poplar (popular).

16   **What trees are left behind after a fire?**
Ashes.

17   **What tree is often found in bottles?**
Cork.

18   **What tree is it that is made of stone?**
Lime.

19   **What tree always is two people?**
Pear (pair).

20   **What tree is a fish?**
Bass(wood).

21   **What tree is the straightest tree that grows?**
Plum (plumb).

22   **What tree is older than most other trees?**
Elder.

23   **What tree is often found in people's mouths?**
Gum.

24   What tree runs over the meadows and pastures?
      Yew (ewe).

25   What tree is an awful grouch?
      Crab.

26   What tree is worn in the Orient?
      Sandal (wood).

27   What tree suggests a color?
      Redwood.

28   What tree suggests a fabric?
      Cotton(wood).

DICTIONARY
NATIONS

1   What nation is a fortune-telling nation?
2   What nation is tough on rats?
3   What nation is a fanciful nation?
4   What nation is dreaded by schoolboys?
5   What nation is a religious nation?
6   What nation is one of the most resolute nations?
7   What nation is a dramatic nation?
8   What nation is one that has come to an end?
9   What nation is a crazy nation?
10   What nation is a political nation?
11   What nation is a bewildered nation?
12   What nation is one that travelers often want?
13   What nation is a disliked nation?
14   What nation is a teacher's nation?
15   What nation is a very bright nation?
16   What nation is a leaning nation?
17   What nation produces the greatest number of marriages?
18   What nation scatters things far and wide?
19   What nation is a tyrant?
20   What is a very unfair nation?
21   What nation is a scheming nation?
22   What nation is at the peak?
23   What nation is a lazy nation?
24   What nation is a disrespectful nation?

1 Divination 2 Extermination 3 Imagination 4 Examination 5 Denomination 6 Determination 7 Impersonation 8 Termination 9 Hallucination 10 Nomination 11 Consternation 12 Destination 13 Abomination 14 Explanation 15 Illumination 16 Inclination 17 Fascination 18 Dissemination 19 Domination 20 Discrimination 21 Machination 22 Culmination 23 Procrastination 24 Insubordination

SEE
ANY
RESEMBLANCE?

1. **Why do good resolutions resemble ladies who faint in church?**
   Because the sooner they are carried out the better.

2. **Why does the Fourth of July resemble an oyster stew?**
   Because we enjoy it most with crackers.

3. **Why does a good gardener resemble a detective-story writer?**
   Because he works hard at his plot.

4. **Why does a hat resemble a king?**
   Because it has a crown.

5. **Why do laws resemble the ocean?**
   Because the most trouble is caused by the breakers.

6. **Why does opening a letter resemble a strange way of entering a room?**
   Because it is breaking through the ceiling (sealing).

7. **Why does a young man trying to raise a moustache resemble a cow's tail?**
   Because he is growing down.

8. **Why does a love of the ocean resemble curiosity?**
   Because it has sent many a boy to sea (see).

9   Why does a pig in a parlor resemble a fire?
Because the sooner it's put out the better.

10   Why does a farmer guiding a plow resemble an ocean liner?
Because one sees the plow, and the other plows the sea.

11   Why does a postage stamp resemble an obstinate donkey?
Because the more you lick it the more it sticks.

12   Why does a New Year's resolution resemble an egg?
Because it is so easily broken.

13   Why does a man riding swiftly uphill resemble one who gives a young dog to his girl-friend?
Because he gives a gallop up (gives a gal a pup).

14   Why does a person with his eyes closed resemble a bad schoolteacher?
Because he keeps his pupils in darkness.

15   Why does your shadow resemble a false friend?
Because it only follows you in sunshine, and deserts you when you're under a cloud.

16   Why does a bootblack resemble the sun?
Because he shines for all.

17   Why does an old man's head resemble a song sung by a very bad singer?
Because it is often terribly bawled (bald).

18   Why does snow resemble a maple tree?
Because it leaves in the early Spring.

19   Why do sentries resemble day and night?
Because when one comes the other goes.

20 Why does an opera singer resemble a drugstore soda jerker?
Because she gives out high screams (ice creams).

21 Why do the fixed stars resemble paper?
Because they are stationary (stationery).

22 Why do stars resemble an old barn?
Because there are R-A-T-S in both of them.

23 Why does sympathy resemble a game of blindman's buff?
Because it is a fellow feeling for a fellow mortal.

24 Why does an oyster resemble a man of good sense?
Because it knows how to keep its mouth shut.

HEADS
I WIN

1   What is a head that glows?
2   What is a head that is bound to have its own way?
3   What is a head that every football player knows?
4   What is a head that pains?
5   What is a head that makes progress?
6   What is a head that's good to eat?
7   What is a head that chases after people to do them no good?
8   What is a head that you see in newspapers?
9   What is a head that is the center of operations?
10 What is a head that seats you in a hotel dining room?
11 What is a head that flows rapidly?
12 What is a head that Indians like to wear?

1 Headlight 2 Headstrong 3 Headgear 4 Headache 5 Headway 6 Headcheese 7 Headhunter 8 Headlines 9 Headquarters 10 Head waiter 11 Headwater 12 Headdress

DOWN THE GARDEN PATH

1   What vegetable is measured like diamonds?
    Carrots (carats).

2   What fruit is never found singly?
    A pear (pair).

3   What vegetable hurts when you step on it?
    Corn.

4   What fruit will shock you if you touch it?
    Currant (current).

5   What vegetable do you find in crowded streetcars
    and buses?
    Squash.

6   What vegetable has the most money in it?
    Mint.

7   What vegetable needs a plumber?
    Leek.

8   What fruit is like a book?
    The strawberry, because it is read (red).

9   What fruit is found on a penny?
    Date.

WHAT'S THE GOOD WORD?

1   What word of six letters contains six words besides itself, without transposing any of its letters?
Herein—he, her, here, ere, rein, in.

2   In what common word does the letter O sound like the letter I?
Women.

3   Can you name two words that begin with P, in which the P is silent?
Psalms; pneumonia.

4   Can you name three common words, each containing a B, in which the B is silent?
Doubt, debt and subtle.

5   Can you name a word containing the letter I, in which the I is silent?
Plaid.

6   What word, by changing the position of one letter, becomes its opposite?
United—untied.

7   What word is it from which the whole may be taken and yet some will be left?
Wholesome.

8   What word of five letters has only one left when two letters are subtracted from it?
St(one).

9   What word, when deprived of one of its letters, makes you sick?
(M)usic.

10   Is there a word in the English language that contains all the vowels?
Unquestionably.

11   In a certain word the letter L is in the middle, in the beginning, and at the end. There is only one L in the word. What is this peculiar word?
The word is "inland." L is in the middle. In is the beginning. And is at the end.

12   What word of five letters has six left after you take two away?
Six-ty.

13   What word of fifteen letters is there from which you can subtract twelve and leave ten?
Pre-ten-tiousness.

14   Can you think of two eight-letter words, one of which has one syllable and the other five syllables?
Strength and ideality.

15   What word of five syllables is it that, if you take away one syllable, no syllable remains?
Monosyllable. Take away mo, and no-syllable remains.

16   Which word in the English language contains the greatest number of letters?
Supercalifragilisticexpialidocious (34 letters).

17   There is a common word of three syllables from which, if you take away five letters, a male will remain. If you take away four letters, a female will

remain. If you take away three, a great man will appear, and the whole word tells you what Joan of Arc was.

Heroine—He, her, hero, heroine.

18   What word of ten letters might be spelled with five?
     Expediency—XPDNC.

19   What words can be pronounced quicker and shorter by adding another syllable to them?
     The words "quick" and "short."

20   What word of eight letters is there from which you can subtract five and leave ten?
     Ten-dency.

21   There are two words in the English language in which the five vowels follow each other in their regular order—A, E, I, O, U. Which words are they?
     Facetious and abstemious.

22   What word of four syllables represents Sin riding on a little animal?
     Synonymous (Sin on a mouse).

23   What is the longest word in the English language?
     Smiles, because there is a mile between its first and last letter.

TURN-AROUND
RIDDLES

The answer to each of the following riddles is found by turning around the letters of the first word to form the second.

1   Can you turn around a portion and get a snare?
    Part—trap.

2   Can you turn around a short sleep and get a kitchen utensil?
    Nap—pan.

3   Can you turn around a well-known kind of cheese and get a word meaning "fabricated"?
    Edam—made.

4   Can you turn around a part of a ship and get a vegetable?
    Keel—leek.

5   Can you turn around a part of a fence and get a prevaricator?
    Rail—liar.

6   Can you turn around a small one-masted sailboat and get little lakes?
    Sloop—pools.

7   Can you turn around fate and get a state of mind?
    Doom—mood.

8   **Can you turn around clever and get English trolley cars?**
Smart—trams.

9   **Can you turn around wicked and get wide-awake?**
Evil—live.

10   **Can you turn around a mouthful and get a stopper?**
Gulp—plug.

11   **Can you turn around a strong, sharp taste and get an insect?**
Tang—gnat.

FLOWER RIDDLES

1   What flower tells what the teacher did when he sat on a tack?
Rose.

2   What flowers does everybody have?
Tulips (two lips).

3   What flower do unmarried men often lose?
Bachelor's buttons.

4   What flower is like a lot of birds?
Phlox (flocks).

5   What flower is like a pretty girl who has had a quarrel with her boy-friend?
Bluebell.

6   What flower represents what the walls of stage castles are made of?
Sham-rock.

7   What flower does every new mother want to listen to?
Baby's breath.

8   What flower do some penniless people hope to do?
Marigold (Marry gold).

9   What flower is an American pin-up girl?
American Beauty.

10   What flower is a wise and experienced person?
Sage.

11   What flower is an eyeful?
Iris.

12   What flower represents a landlord who shuts off the heat?
Freesia (freeze you).

13   What flower resembles a tattered bird?
Ragged robin.

14   What flower is just the thing for a girl to wear to a party?
Lady's slipper.

15   What flower reminds you of teatime?
Four o'clock.

16   What flower is a dressed-up wild animal?
Dandelion (dandy lion).

17   What flower is a church official?
Elder.

18   What flower resembles the rising sun?
Morning glory.

19   What flower is a dear boy?
Sweet William.

20   What flower is what pa did when he proposed to ma?
Aster (asked her).

21   What flower is most used by cooks?
Buttercup.

22   What flower is a parting remark to a friend?
Forget-me-not.

23   What flower is worn by the fishermen of Holland?
Dutchman's breeches.

24   What flower goes with the easy chair and the paper?
Dutchman's pipe.

25   What flower is both pleasant and distasteful at the same time?
Bittersweet.

26   What flower reminds you of winter weather?
Snowdrop.

27   What flower tells what George Washington was to his country?
Poppy.

28   What flower suggests neat lines?
Primrose (prim rows).

29   What flower suggests a feline bite?
Cat-nip.

30   What flower is a boy's delight in winter?
Snowball.

31   If a mercenary man were to ask a girl to marry him, what flower might he name?
Anemone (any money)?

32   What is it that is very queer about flowers?
They shoot before they have pistols (pistils).

33   What flower most resembles a bull's mouth?
A cowslip (cow's lip).

34   What flower do television comedians often rely on?
Cornflower.

SOME
HARD NUTS
TO CRACK

1. **What nut is found beside the sea?**
    Beechnut.

2. **What nut is a slow-burning nut?**
    Candlenut.

3. **What nut is the staff of life?**
    Breadnut.

4. **What nut is a hot drink?**
    Coconut.

5. **What nut is an uncooked-bread nut?**
    Doughnut.

6. **What nut is made from a product of cows?**
    Butternut.

7. **What nut is a girl's name?**
    Hazelnut.

8. **What nut is part of a room?**
    Walnut (wall nut).

9. **What nut is a vegetable?**
    Peanut.

10   **What nut is a box?**
Chestnut.

11   **What nut is a South American country?**
Brazil nut.

12   **What nut sounds like a sneeze?**
Cashew nut.

13   **Why are a walnut and a regiment of soldiers alike?**
Because they both have a kernel (colonel).

14   **Did you hear about the big accident down at the railroad station?**
A train ran over a peanut, a shell exploded, and two kernels (colonels) were crushed.

15   **What nut has neither shell nor kernel and does not grow on a tree?**
Doughnut.

LET 'ER RIDE!

1 What two letters express the words "not difficult"?
EZ (easy).

2 What two letters express the word "deteriorate"?
DK (decay).

3 What number and letter describe a popular outdoor game?
10 S (tennis).

4 What two letters describe that which exceeds the required amount?
XS (excess).

5 What three letters describe a foe?
NME (enemy).

6 What three letters give the name of a midwestern state?
IOA (Iowa).

7 What two letters and a number mean to turn aside?
DV8 (deviate).

8 What two letters name a climbing plant?
IV (ivy).

9 What three letters and a number mean relieve?
LEV8 (alleviate).

10 What two letters describe a wormlike fish?
EL (eel).

11 What three letters spell something that exists?
NTT (entity).

12 What two letters spell barren or bare?
MT (empty).

13 What one letter and a number describe a dog?
K9 (canine).

14 What two letters spell a word meaning jealousy?
NV (envy).

15 What two letters spell a number less than one hundred?
AT (eighty).

16 What three letters and a number describe a person who flies an airplane?
AV8R (aviator).

17 What two letters describe a kind of light gun?
BB.

18 What two letters spell a word that means "having to do with art"?
RT (arty).

19 What four letters spell a title given to high diplomatic officials?
XLNC (Excellency).

20 What one number and one letter spell a raid against the enemy?
4A (foray).

21   What two letters spell a girl's name?
KT, LN and LC (Katie, Ellen and Elsie).

22   What number and letter spell anticipate?
4C (foresee).

23   What are the most forcible three letters in the alphabet?
NRG (energy).

24   What two letters spell to do better?
XL (excel).

25   What letter and number spell conquered?
B 10 (beaten).

26   What letter and number spell having finished a meal?
E 10 (eaten).

27   What two letters spell a word meaning some?
NE (any).

28   What two letters spell a word meaning try to do?
SA (essay).

29   What letter and number mean ahead of or in front of?
B 4 (before).

30   What two letters and a number mean to flow forth?
MN 8 (emanate).

31   What two letters spell an attractive girl?
QT (cutie).

32   What two letters spell a cotton fabric?
PK (pique).

33   What two letters spell shabby or ragged?
CD (seedy).

34   What two letters spell a seat in church?
PU (pew).

35   What two letters spell chilly?
IC (icy).

36   What two letters spell an Indian tent?
TP (tepee).

37   What two letters spell results?
FX (effects).

38   What three letters spell great happiness?
XTC (ecstasy).

39   What three letters spell a funeral poem?
LEG (elegy).

40   What letters spell not dumb?
Y's (wise).

41   What three letters spell a poet's place of simple pleasures?
RKD (arcady).

42   What letters spell comfort?
E's (ease).

43   What two letters and a number spell a drug?
OP8 (opiate).

44   What letters spell a great deal of water?
C's (seas).

45   What letters spell what bad boys do?
T's (tease).

46   What five letters spell advisability?
XPDNC (expediency).

47 What two letters are a hot condiment?
    KN (cayenne).

48 What two letters spell an English county?
    SX (Essex).

49 Like which four letters of the alphabet is a honey-
    producing insect when he is not feeling too well?
    ACDB (a seedy bee).

50 How would you say in two letters that you were twice
    as heavy as a friend?
    IW (I double you).

WATCH YOUR STEP!

1   What part of a watch supports a flower?
    Stem.

2   What part of a watch was used before by somebody
    else?
    Second hand.

3   What does a watch mark that is read by the secre-
    tary at a meeting?
    Minutes.

4   What part of a watch is something that a tight-rope
    walker is good at?
    Balance wheel.

5   What part of a watch is used as tableware?
    Crystal.

6   What part of a watch is what the palmist studies?
    Hands.

7   What part of a watch do we use when we greet some-
    one?
    Hour hand.

8   What part of a watch do women love for ornaments?
    Jewels.

9   What part of a watch will always give you a cool drink?
Spring.

10   What part of a watch sometimes, according to certain people, stops a clock?
Face.

11   Why is modesty the strongest characteristic of a watch?
Because it always keeps its hands before its face and runs down its own works.

12   Why is a watch like a river?
Because it won't run long without winding.

13   Why should a man always wear a watch when he travels in a desert?
Because every watch has a spring in it.

14   Why can't a thief steal a watch very easily?
Because he must take it off its guard.

15   Why are the hours from one to twelve like good policemen?
Because they are always on the watch.

16   What is it that has a face, but no head; hands, but no feet; yet travels everywhere and is usually running?
A watch.

RIDDLES IN RHYME

1 Round as a biscuit, busy as a bee,
   Prettiest little thing you ever did see.
   A watch.

2 A houseful, a roomful,
   Can't catch a spoonful.
   Smoke.

3 What runs, but does not walk,
   Has a tongue, but can't talk?
   A wagon.

4 What is deep as a house.
   And round as a cup,
   And all the king's horses
   Can't draw it up?
   A well.

5 Four jolly men sat down to play,
   And played all night ti'l break of day;
   They played for cash and not for fun,
   With separate scores for everyone,
   Yet when they came to square accounts,
   They all had made quite fair amounts.
   Can you this paradox explain?
   If no one lost, how could all gain?
   The four players were musicians in a
   dance orchestra.

6   I'm the name of a country, and strange, you'll declare,
If you cut off my head, why, I am still there.
Take away my tail twice, but nought you will gain,
For e'en though you do, I still will remain.
What country am I?

Siam. Cut off its head—S—and "I am" is still there.
Then, take away A and M, and I still remains.

7   The mother of men was a lady whose name
Read backward or forward, is always the same.

Eve.

8   Sometimes I am very sly,
Other times a trade I ply;
Over the billows swift I fly,
Now, pray tell me, who am I?

Craft.

9   Thirty-two white horses on a red hill,
Now they go, and now they stand still.

Your teeth.

10   What does a man love more than life?
Hate more than death or mortal strife?
That which contented men desire,
The poor have, the rich require;
The miser spends, the spendthrift saves,
And all men carry to their graves?

Nothing.

11   As I was going to St. Ives,
I chanced to meet nine old wives;
Each wife had nine sacks,
Each sack had nine cats,
Each cat had nine kits.
Kits, cats, sacks and wives,
How many were going to St. Ives?

Only one. The old wives were going in the
opposite direction.

12   Little Nanny Etticote, in a white petticoat,
          Holding up a bright red rose;
          The longer she stands, the shorter she grows.

A candle.

13   Behind the barn at early morn
          I heard a herald blow his horn.
          His beard was flesh, his mouth was horn,
          The like of him was never born.

A rooster. (Roosters are hatched, not born.)

14   'Tis true I have both face and hands,
          And move before your eye;
          Yet when I go my body stands,
          And when I stand, I lie.

A clock.

15   I claim no magic power,
          Yet a fast I can make a feast.
          I am never among the first,
          But the last I can make the least.

          The gust of the wildest storm
          I can change to a welcome guest,
          In the North or the South I'm unknown,
          But am found in the East or the West.

The letter E.

16   I tell heat, and I tell cold,
          And they in turn tell me
          To go up and down as I am told
          They tell me; I agree.

The mercury in a thermometer.

17   When walking through a field of wheat,
          I picked up something good to eat,
          'Twas neither fish, flesh, fowl nor bone;
          I kept it till it ran alone.

An egg that hatched into a chicken.

18   I'm a feeling all persons detest,
Although I'm by everyone felt;
By two letters I'm fully expressed.
But by twice two I always am spelled.

NV—envy.

19   There's a word that's composed of three letters
        alone,
Which reads backward and forward the same;
It expresses the sentiments warm from the heart,
And to beauty lays principal claim.

Eye.

20   Part of a foot with judgment transpose,
And the answer you'll find just under your nose.

Inch—chin.

21   Legs I have, but seldom walk;
I backbite all, yet never talk.

A flea.

22   You saw me where I never was,
And where I could not be;
And yet within that very place,
My face you often see.

A reflection in the mirror.

23   There was a man who was not born,
His father was not before him;
He did not live, he did not die,
His epitaph is not o'er him.
Who could this have been?

A man whose name was Nott.

24   Your initials begin with an A,
You've an A at the end of your name.
The whole of your name is an A,
And it's backward and forward the same.

Anna.

25 Old Mother Twitchhead had but one eye,
    And a long tail, which she let fly;
    Every time she went over a gap,
    She left a bit of her tail in a trap.
    A needle and thread.

26 Those who take me improve, be their task what it
        may,
    Those who have me are sorrowful through the long
        day;
    I am hated alike by the foolish and wise,
    Yet without me none ever to eminence rise.
    Pains.

27 Adam and Eve and Pinch Me
    Went down to the river to bathe;
    Adam and Eve were drowned,
    And who do you think was saved?
    Pinch Me! (When your friend answers "Pinch me," go
    right ahead and pinch him, since he asked for it.)

28 Up and down, up and down,
    Touching neither sky nor ground.
    A pump handle.

29 Instead of complaining when it may rain,
    We should do as they do in Spain.
    And what is that?
    Let it rain.

30 It wasn't my sister, nor my brother,
    But still was the child of my father and mother.
    Who was it?
    Myself.

31 We travel much, yet prisoners are,
    And close confined, to boot,
    We with the swiftest horse keep pace,
    Yet always go on foot.
    A pair of spurs.

32   I often murmur, but never weep;
            Lie in bed, but never sleep;
            My mouth is larger than my head,
            In spite of the fact I'm never fed;
            I have no feet, yet swiftly run;
            The more falls I get, move faster on.
            A river.

33   Unable to think, unable to speak,
            Yet I tell the truth to all who peek.
            A pair of scales.

34   Though I dance at a ball,
            I am nothing at all.
            A shadow.

35   Great numbers do our use despise,
            But yet, at last they find,
            Without our help in many things,
            They might as well be blind.
            A pair of spectacles.

36   If a well-known animal you behead,
            Another one you will have instead.
            F—ox.

37   Ever running on my race,
            Never staying at one place,
            Through the world I make my tour,
            Everywhere at the same hour.
            If you please to spell my name,
            Backward and forward, it's the same.
            Noon.

38   What is it that no man ever yet did see,
            Which never was, but always is to be?
            Tomorrow.

39   I can throw an egg against the wall,
            And it will neither break nor fall.
            How is this?
            The wall won't either break or fall.

40 I tremble at each breath of air,
And yet the heaviest burdens bear.
Water.

41 Three of us in six, and five of us in seven,
Four of us in nine, and six in eleven.
Letters.

42 It shoots you when you're looking,
It shoots you when you're not.
This candid instrument, indeed,
Can put you on the spot.
A camera.

43 No need for brush, no need for broom,
I'm used a lot to tidy a room.
A vacuum cleaner.

44 You can press your attire,
When I contact a wire.
An electric iron.

45 What is it you can touch,
And also you can feel;
It has neither size nor shape,
But just the same, it's real.
The air.

ADAM AND EVE AND THE APPLE

This is a famous but rather complicated riddle.

A group of friends were discussing the subject of how many apples Adam and Eve ate in the Garden of Eden. The first person to speak was very matter-of-fact and said that it could only have been one apple.

The second person asserted that Adam 8 and Eve ate 2, making a total of 10.

The third person said there was something wrong with that, because Eve 8 and Adam 8 also, making 16.

"But," said another person, "if Eve 8 and Adam 82, that would be a total of 90."

Still another person said: "According to history, Eve 81 and Adam 82. That would total 163."

"But," put in someone else, "don't you see that if Eve 81 and Adam 812, that would make a total of 893."

"According to my figuring," said a college professor, "if Eve 814 Adam and Adam 8124 Eve, that would total 8938."

At that point, they all gave up.

DICTIONARY

CITIES

1   What is an odd city?
2   What is a weak city?
3   What is a measuring city?
4   What is a lighted city?
5   What is a savage city?
6   What is a very bad city?
7   What is a greedy city?
8   What is a very fast city?
9   What is a bold city?
10   What is a fast-developing city?
11   What is a happy city?
12   What is a quarrelsome city?
13   What is a truthful city?
14   What is a resilient city?
15   What is a genuine city?
16   What is a discerning city?
17   What is a wise city?
18   What is a rural city?
19   What is a false city?
20   What is an advertiser's city?
21   What is a homey city?
22   What is a hypocritical city?

1 Eccentricity   2 Incapacity   3 Capacity   4 Electricity
5 Ferocity   6 Atrocity   7 Rapacity   8 Velocity
9 Audacity   10 Precocity   11 Felicity   12 Pugnacity
13 Veracity   14 Elasticity   15 Authenticity   16 Perspicacity   17 Sagacity   18 Rusticity   19 Mendacity
20 Publicity   21 Domesticity   22 Duplicity

BIRD
BAFFLERS

1   What bird is a letter?
Jay.

2   What bird is essential to eating?
Swallow.

3   What bird is a high dignitary of the church?
Cardinal.

4   What bird is a chessman?
Rook.

5   What good bird deserves another?
Tern (turn).

6   What two birds are foolish?
Loons and cuckoos.

7   What bird is a name?
Robin.

8   What bird is getting run over all the time?
Rail.

9   What bird can lift the heaviest weight?
Crane.

10   **What is the rudest bird?**
Mockingbird.

11   **How do we know that nightingales are very gay birds?**
Because they have a high time after dark.

12   **How do canary birds pay their debts?**
By giving their notes.

13   **When is a pigeon like a drinking glass?**
When it's a tumbler.

14   **Which bird is the lowest-spirited?**
Bluebird.

15   **What bird is it that is found in Africa, and though it has wings, can't fly?**
A dead one.

ABBREVIATED STATES

1   What state is a number?
          Tenn.

2   What state is a doctor?
          Md.

3   What state always seems to be in poor health?
          Ill.

4   What state serves as a source of metal?
          Ore.

5   What state is the cleanest?
          Wash.

6   What state is as good as a mile?
          Miss.

7   What state is to cut long grass?
          Mo.

8   What state never forgets itself?
          Me.

9   What state is Moslem?
          Ala.

10   What state saved Noah and his family?
      Ark.

11   What state is an exclamation?
      O.

12   What state is a grain?
      R.I. (Rye).

13   What state is a fond parent?
      Pa.

14   What state is to study carefully?
      Conn. (Con).

15   What state is the happiest?
      Ga. (Gay).

TRANSPOSED TREES

The following words can be rearranged to spell the names of trees. What trees are they?

1	Mile	7	Cared
2	North	8	Cheap
3	Panes	9	Mug
4	Clouts	10	Reap
5	Ample	11	Melon
6	Has	12	Lamp
		13	Lump

1 Lime 2 Thorn 3 Aspen 4 Locust 5 Maple 6 Ash
7 Cedar 8 Peach 9 Gum 10 Pear 11 Lemon
12 Palm 13 Plum

A PENNY
FOR
YOUR
THOUGHTS

1   What is on a penny that is part of a nail?
     Head.

2   What is on a penny that is part of a hill?
     Brow.

3   What is on a penny that Patrick Henry wanted?
     Liberty.

4   What is on a penny that is slang for conversation?
     Chin.

5   What is on a penny that is part of a needle?
     Eye.

6   What is it on a penny that means in favor of, and to
     rasp?
     Pro-file.

7   What is on a penny that is a narrow piece of land?
     A neck.

8   What are on a penny that are found in post offices?
     Letters.

9   What is on a penny that is part of a river?
     Mouth.

10 What is on a penny that "fresh" people have?
    Cheek.

11 What is on a penny that understands?
    Nose (knows).

12 What is on a penny that is a messenger?
    One sent (cent).

13 What is on a penny that is an ancient weapon?
    Bow.

14 What is on a penny that is part of a book?
    Leaves.

15 What is on a penny that is a policeman?
    Copper.

16 What is on a penny that is a big industrial combi-
    nation?
    Trust.

17 What is on a penny that is one-third of the world's
    land surface?
    America.

18 What is on a penny that is like being married?
    United.

19 What is on a penny that is a book of the Bible?
    Numbers.

KATE'S
A GOOD
SKATE

1   What Kate talks and writes a lot?
Communicate.

2   What Kate makes things invisible?
Eradicate.

3   What Kate is twins?
Duplicate.

4   What Kate is always showing the way?
Indicate.

5   What Kate finds things for you?
Locate.

6   What Kate can't breathe?
Suffocate.

7   What Kate likes school?
Educate.

8   What Kate is in many newspapers?
Syndicate.

9   What Kate is full of advice?
Advocate.

10   What Kate is good at getting out of tight places?
     Extricate.

11   What Kate keeps the machinery going smoothly?
     Lubricate.

12   What Kate is inclined to be sickly?
     Delicate.

13   What Kate is always chewing on something?
     Masticate.

14   What Kate is clever at predicting things?
     Prognosticate.

15   What Kate consecrates things?
     Dedicate.

16   What Kate gives up the throne?
     Abdicate.

17   What two Kates tell fibs?
     Fabricate and Prevaricate.

18   What Kate is a good peacemaker?
     Placate.

19   What Kate is always leaving places?
     Vacate.

20   What Kate justifies people?
     Vindicate.

21   What Kate is always disapproving?
     Deprecate.

22   What Kate gets people in trouble?
     Implicate.

11   What Kate keeps the machinery going smoothly?
      Lubricate.

RIDDLES WITH DUMB ENDINGS

1   **What is dumb but knowing?**
     Wisdom.

2   **What is dumb but liberty-loving?**
     Freedom.

3   **What is dumb and also tiresome?**
     Boredom.

4   **What is dumb and infrequent?**
     Seldom.

5   **What is dumb but full of high public officers?**
     Officialdom.

6   **What is dumb but sacrifices itself for ideals?**
     Martyrdom.

7   **What is dumb and ruled by a powerful monarch?**
     Kingdom.

JUST
DUCKY

1   **Why does a duck go in the water?**
For diverse (diver's) reasons.

2   **Why does he come out?**
For sundry (sun—dry) reasons.

3   **What does every duckling become when it first takes to the water?**
It becomes wet.

4   **Why does a duck who needs some money come out of the water?**
To make a run on the bank.

5   **When a farm woman was asked how many ducks she had, she replied: "As they all ran down the path, I saw there was a duck in front of two ducks, a duck behind two ducks, and a duck between two ducks." How many ducks were there?**
Three ducks, one after the other.

6   **What is the difference between a duck with one wing and one with two?**
Merely a difference of a pinion (opinion).

7   **What is the difference between a man dodging boots that are being thrown at him and a man chasing a flock of ducks out of his pond?**
One ducks the shoes, and the other shoos the ducks.

DO YOU KNOW YOUR AUNTS?

1   **What aunt is a traveling aunt?**
    Itinerant.

2   **What aunt is a sweet-smelling aunt?**
    Fragrant.

3   **What aunt is a despotic aunt?**
    Tyrant.

4   **What aunt is a vagabond aunt?**
    Vagrant.

5   **What aunt is a schoolteacher aunt?**
    Pedant.

6   **What aunt is a hard, unyielding aunt?**
    Adamant.

7   **What aunt is a zestful aunt?**
    Piquant.

8   **What aunt is a conspicuous aunt?**
    Flagrant.

9   **What aunt is a dangerous aunt?**
    Malignant.

10   **What aunt is a bossy aunt?**
      Dominant.

11   **What aunt is a calculating aunt?**
      Accountant.

12   **What aunt is always put out about something?**
      Indignant.

13   **What aunt is an uninformed aunt?**
      Ignorant.

14   **What aunt is a beggar aunt?**
      Mendicant.

15   **What aunt is a prevailing aunt?**
      Predominant.

16   **What aunt is an inharmonious aunt?**
      Discordant.

17   **What aunt is an impertinent aunt?**
      Flippant.

18   **What aunt makes good jelly?**
      Currant.

19   **What aunt is like a still pond?**
      Stagnant.

20   **What are the biggest kind of aunts?**
      Giants.

21   **What aunt provides a place for you to eat?**
      Restaurant.

REAL

CITIES

1	What city is a sofa?
2	What city is a very hard substance?
3	What city is found in the library?
4	What city is a kind of paper?
5	What city is an improvement on Noah's boat?
6	What city is a small stone?
7	What city is a good cigar?
8	What city is a briny body of water?
9	What city is a perfume?
10	What city is a famous President?
11	What city likes to wander about?
12	What city is a place on which to play a game?

1 Davenport 2 Flint 3 Reading 4 Manila 5 Newark
6 Little Rock 7 Havana 8 Salt Lake City 9 Cologne
10 Lincoln (or Washington) 11 Rome 12 Bowling
Green

JACKS
OF ALL
TRADES

1   **What Jack is a woodsman?**
Lumberjack.

2   **What Jack has a head but no body?**
Jack-o-Lantern.

3   **What Jack paints people's windows?**
Jack Frost.

4   **What Jack's name takes too long to say?**
Jack Robinson.

5   **What Jacks do most of us wear?**
Jackets.

6   **What Jack is performed in diving?**
Jackknife.

7   **What Jack helps to remove foot coverings?**
Bootjack.

8   **What Jack flies on a British ship?**
Union Jack.

9   **What Jack is a whiz?**
Crackerjack.

10   **What Jack resembles a wolf?**
Jackal.

11   **What Jack is a terrible disease?**
Yellowjack.

12   **What Jack has no legs but jumps?**
Jack-in-the box.

13   **What Jack is always a sailor?**
Jack tar.

14   **What Jack has strings?**
Jumping jack.

15   **What Jack tastes good with syrup?**
Flapjack.

16   **What Jack has long ears and a white tail?**
Jackrabbit.

17   **What Jack do we seldom hit?**
Jackpot.

TRICKS OF THE TRADES

1   What trade does the sun follow?
     Tanner.

2   What trade does the President follow?
     Cabinet-maker.

3   Of what trade is a man whose best works are always
     trampled on?
     Shoemaker.

4   Of what trade can it be said that all its members are
     men of letters?
     Printing trade.

5   What trade is best qualified to cook a rabbit?
     Hairdressers (hare dressers).

6   What trade is noted among the authors of English
     literature?
     Goldsmith.

7   Of what trade is the preacher at a wedding?
     Joiner.

THE BISHOP'S RIDDLE

A famous old riddle is said to have been made up by the English Bishop Wilberforce. Here is his riddle:

I am a wonderful trunk, which contains the following articles: 1 A box. 2 Two lids. 3 Two musical instruments. 4 A number of articles that are indispensable to a carpenter. 5 Two tropical trees. 6 Two good fish. 7 A number of shellfish. 8 A fine stag. 9 A number of small animals, swift and shy. 10 Two playful animals. 11 Weapons of warfare. 12 Steps of a hotel. 13 Some whips without handles. 14 Two learners. 15 The upper edge of a hill. 16 A number of weathercocks. 17 Two established measures. 18 Two sides of a vote. 19 Fine flowers. 20 A fruit. 21 Two places of worship. 22 A possible remark of Nebuchadnezzar when eating grass. 23 Ten Spanish noblemen. 24 A desert place. 25 Part of a bell. 26 A garden vegetable. 27 An isthmus.

> The trunk is the human body. It contains: 1 Chest. 2 Eyelids. 3 Eardrums. 4 Nails. 5 Palms. 6 Soles. 7 Muscles (mussels). 8 Heart (hart). 9 Hairs (hares). 10 Calves. 11 Arms. 12 Insteps (inn steps). 13 Lashes. 14 Pupils. 15 Brow. 16 Veins (vanes). 17 Feet and hands. 18 Eyes and nose (ayes and noes). 19 Two lips (tulips). 20 Adam's apple. 21 Temples. 22 Eyebrows. (I browse). 23 Tendons (ten dons). 24 Waist (waste). 25 Tongue. 26 Pulse. 27 Neck (of land).

FOR
BIGGER,
BETTER
OR WORSE

1 A man named Bigger got married. How did he compare in size with his wife?
He was larger, for he always had been Bigger.

2 Mrs. Bigger had a baby. Now who was bigger?
The baby, because he was a little Bigger.

3 Mr. Bigger died. Then who was bigger?
Mrs. Bigger, for she was Bigger still.

4 What is better than to give credit where credit is due?
Give cash.

5 What is better than presence of mind in a railroad accident?
Absence of body.

6 What is worse than raining cats and dogs?
Hailing buses.

7 What is worse than a giraffe with a sore throat?
A centipede with sore feet.